A Funny Old Sailor

Books should be returned on or before the
last date stamped below

1 7 FEB 2007

~ 1 NOV 2008

2 4 FEB 2009

2 4 MAR 2009

~ 2010

5 JAN 2011

2 6 JAN 2011

1 9 MAR 2011

2 2 JUN 2011

1 9 MAR 2012

1 6 MAR 2013

1 6 JUL 2013

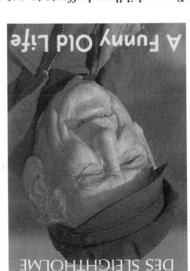

DES SLEIGHTHOLME

A Funny Old Life

A forerunner to *A Funny Old Sailor, A Funny Old Life* is the wonderfully entertaining nautobiography of one of the best known and best loved characters of the sailing world.

Des Sleightholme, former Editor of *Yachting Monthly* for many years, is well known for his irreverent outlook on the Establishment and for his unfailing eye for the funny side of things; here he takes us on a hilarious anecdotal romp through his sailing life.

From childhood efforts to get afloat at all costs – 'if it floats stand on it' – to the tribulations of running a charter boat, the wandering narrative moves from the high drama of a force ten dismasting to the farce of a shattered toilet bowl.

Des Sleightholme has always had a connoisseur's eye for a cock-up. In *A Funny Old Life* he mercilessly sends up both himself and the poor unfortunates with whom he has come in contact over the years.

'Des Sleightholme is one of the few genuinely funny yachting writers.' Andrew Bray, *Yachting World*

'There are really only two slide-splitting yachting journalists operating today – one of them is J D Sleightholme.' *Dolphin Book Club*

'What a cracking book this is.' *Sailing*

A Funny Old Sailor

Further anecdotes
from the life of
Des Sleightholme

Illustrations by the author

Des Sleightholme

ADLARD COLES NAUTICAL
London

Published by Adlard Coles Nautical
an imprint of A & C Black Publishers Ltd
37 Soho Square, London W1D 3QZ
www.adlardcoles.com

First edition 2003

ISBN 0 7136 6713 3

A CIP catalogue record for this book is available from the British Library.

A & C Black uses paper produced with elemental chlorine-free pulp,
harvested from managed sustainable forests.

Typeset in 10½ on 12½pt Garamond Book
Printed and bound in Great Britain by
Cromwell Press, Trowbridge, Wilts

Contents

Foreword

You know what it's like when you're on passage. You come off watch totally bushed and flake out down below on the lee settee. You sigh and close your eyes. Then you open them again because you're suddenly wide, wide awake and any hope of sleep is remote. So you read a book instead, *any* book, be it Tolstoy's *War and Peace* or Jilly Cooper with a full head of steam. Then...

'You're on!' yells a voice and a pint mug of tea is thrust into your fist, which is when you discover that you've only got halfway down the first page which is now soggy, having absorbed two hours' worth of dribbled saliva.

Finding my roots.
There was this farm called Sleightholme on
Sleightholme moor above Sleightholme beck. 'I'll
surprise them!' I thought. A woman in a flat cap
and sacking was worming a calf. I introduced
myself. 'Oh ah,' she said.

It is with this end in mind that I commend this book. It is a major work of banality – a collection of personal experiences as a boy and as a charter yacht skipper, yachting journalist and mud-yachtsman. It is intellectually undemanding and instantly put-downable. I have inflated it with journalistic puff and flummery to make it reach book-length, otherwise I could have got the whole damn lot into one chapter.

I hope that readers may find the book, well – absorbing.

Des Sleightholme
Hope Cove, Devon

1

A Hard Bit
A blow to the musical world

In 1928 I almost learned to play the fiddle. It was a damn close shave.

Mother was a piano teacher and I was her star failure. I got as far as a number called *Here we go* before she jacked it in. She said that 'I had it in me' though, and shaken but undaunted she bought me this little violin about the size of a meat pasty, plus a bow, a lump of resin and a silk handkerchief to tuck under my chin, which was what you did.

Father played the violin worse than anybody else in Yorkshire. When he was sawing away flat out it was like watching half a sword fight. The bridge was bust so he'd repaired it with a bit of my Meccano. He kept up a running commentary while he was playing. 'By,' he'd say in Yorkshire, 'that were a hard bit!' or, 'Eee, this is a tricky passage!' implying rocks and an exacting bit of navigation.

Mother did a straight deal with a violin teacher called Mrs Lamb who had a circular and sausage-fingered daughter called Elsie, with about as much music in her soul as a workhouse duff has currants. Elsie was to learn the piano and Mrs Lamb would teach me the violin.

My father in drag. He was to become a black treacle eating bird-watching tenor with a chronic sniff. 'Stop that Percy!' mother used to say.

1

Mrs Lamb was vast, her hair was done up in sort of earmuffs, and she seemed to be clad in floaty chiffon scarves and BO. She had this enormous bust and when she bent over me it was like wearing saddle-bags. She'd grip my fingers on my bow and say, 'Firrrm as a little rock Desmond!' and I'd be scarlet-faced with trying to hold my breath while sandwiched between those huge Bristols like a hamburger in a Big Mac. I should have had a side order of french fries.

Mother wasn't getting much joy out of Elsie either. Her great fat fingers could only span about four notes. Like me before her, she got as far as *Here we go* and went no further. Elsie wasn't happy, mother wasn't happy, Mrs Lamb wasn't happy and I sure as hell wasn't. I told mum about the BO and that did it. She flogged the fiddle and I went back to thumping my tin drum.

Well OK, I was a disappointment to my musical parents who doubtless saw me as a child prodigy, buzzing and whining away on my fiddle like a hornet's nest. I might even have become a gypsy fiddler with throbbing arpeggios. Men with throbbing arpeggios are not to be trifled with.

Years rolled by. I was living aboard this small, ex-Morecambe prawner up a creek. She had sitting headroom like living in a storm drain and she was berthed in a haunt of dab-chick and grebe, which I was daft enough to mention to father, who was a twitcher and scatty as tin trousers. 'Oh, I'll come for the weekend,' he said.

He brought his violin and my heart sank like a brick duck. He took in the lack of headroom. 'I may have problems over my stance,' he said. I left him to it all day, spending a fair bit of it killing time in The Sloop.

My only neighbour in the creek was a laconic ex-submariner living on an old MGB and writing his memoirs. I hoped he wouldn't spot my father, but he did. He was waiting to catch me on my return, and grinning like a split sack, he jerked his head towards the prawner from whence came hellish squawks and squeaks.

'I reckon you should get him a bigger cage!' he said.

The prawner had the usual skylight like a garden cold frame with hinge-up glass and bars. Father had stuck his head up into it like some curious exhibit. His music was propped up outside on deck and he was holding his Meccano-modified fiddle at genital level, sawing away as if felling a tree. He saw me coming.

'By,' he said, 'that was a hard bit!'

A Fair Deal
You'd have to go a long way to find a better bargain

Oh I must go down to the sea again,
But first I must settle a doubt;
As I live in Southend it will all depend;
Is the tide in or out?

E very teenage lad should have a tore-out wooden boat which can
only be kept afloat by a succession of tar-and-canvas tingles and
a muddy creek in which to float (or sink) her. This would solve the
youth-crime problem at a stroke (preferably a breast-stroke), the pigs
of ballast carried by way of maintaining the boat in an upright
posture having taken her to the bottom.

When father, leading the way with his tool-box like some latter-
day Moses, led us to the Isle of Wight, I found The Promised Land and
Micky Mouse. She was advertised for two quid as a craftsman-built
rowing skiff. I cashed in the five bob birthday postal orders and
bought her.

It was the worst investment of my life to date. The craftsman
turned out to be a maker of kitchen furniture, and his invisible
scarphs and dovetails were misplaced zeal. As a plywood coffin it
might have had a certain cachet, but he knew nothing of boat
design. Seven feet long, the hull was narrow for speed and high-sided
to keep out the water. Her builder pointed out these features with
pride.

'What's that bolted underneath?' I queried, pointing to the six-
foot hunk of steam-pipe.

'Stability son. That's where you get your stiffness,' he explained
patiently. I was to learn that being dead was the other way to achieve
this quality. I bought, launched – mercifully in two feet of water – and
instantly capsized *Mickey Mouse*. By sawing a six inch slice from
bow to stern in the horizontal plane, I converted her to a topless and

4

instantly swampable kayak and a seven-foot plywood hoss-collar which was totally useless.

Then I met 'Spoofer' Murray and The Creek, acquired a fourteen-foot derelict that spouted leaks like a bidet and was equipped with odd oars and began to learn.

One of the first things I learned was that Spoofer was averse to rowing. Even rowing tandem was unacceptable and his pull would grow weaker and weaker like the death of fairy Tinkerbell. He had, he told me been a poorly child and 'they' had 'almost lost him', implying a search of the bushes and the use of tracker dogs. So he scanned ahead while I stood up and push-rowed.

We were looking for usable flotsum, especially on the big spring tides. The creek would expand, brim to bursting point and allow boats to be propelled, hissing through the grass, to the very limits and beyond, a point determined by the owners of private properties who cupped hands and yelled in a daunting manner.

Thus we found this baulk of timber. It was twice the size of a railway sleeper and mahogany. We appropriated it and went in search of a purchaser.

'Worth a couple of quid, easy!' Spoof said.

At the mouth of the creek there was 'Sticky' Watson's yard. Sticky – the nickname referred to his length of leg – actually built boats, and it seemed likely that our baulk had originated at his yard in the first place. This was a theory we were not keen to put to the test. The other possible purchaser was Derek who had a clanking corrugated iron shed up-creek, and who 'did up' boats.

Derek would restore and sell boats long after all hope of revival had been abandoned by others. He had the artistic skills of the mortician, who with the aid of lipstick, eyeliner and a touch of blusher plus the front half of a double-breasted suit, can restore a cadaver to an appearance of robust health. Derek's restorations used large quantities of builder's cement. Going alongside at speed was inadvisable.

With our baulk in tow, me heaving on the sweeps and Spoofer in his usual figurehead position giving directions, we laid alongside Derek's wobbly jetty. He was down in a flash like a boiler-suited spider summoned by luckless fly and vibrating web – an apt enough simile considering the state of that jetty.

'How about this?' Spoofer opened, jerking his head at the baulk.

It was plain to see that Derek was interested, covetous in fact.

'Oh deary me, that's a rough old bit of stuff!' the old bastard said.

'Three quid,' Spoof told him.

Derek laughed uproariously, 'I like a lad with a sense o' humour. Tell you what we'll do to take it orft your hands. Come along o' me lads, and I'll show you something!'

We followed him up into his shed wherein he had a sort of glassed-in corner with a door that served as an office. He rummaged and produced a gun. It was plainly of antique design with a curly trigger, a wood-worm decimated stock, rusty as a drainpipe and with much the same size bore. He hefted it.

'Took this orf a gent's hands as part-payment for services rendered,' he told us, implying an act of Christian compassion.

'Genuine antique, dealers would knock you down to git their hands on it. Rub up with a bit o' wire wool and she'll come up like new, lads. I ain't got time otherwise...' And he broke off, leaving us with an impression of industry frustrated.

We'd be reckoning on a quick sale.

'Look at this lovely trigger action,' Derek invited, cocking the gun. 'Why, I can even let you have some percussion nipples,' he went on. He rummaged in a drawer and produced a brown paper bag from which he selected a little copper cap and placed it appropriately on the weapon.

Then it happened.

There was a tremendous roar and a jet of flame. The entire upper half of the office door vanished. The row must have been heard all over the village. Dogs barked.

Derek just stood there, face white as paper, holding his still-smoking piece of ordnance, sort of swaying.

'We'll take it!' Spoof said.

Facts of Life
A nice turn of speed and forget the women

W hen I was twelve years of age, mother said I was out-growing my strength which sounded ominous to me, I looked like scaffolding in trousers, father's trousers which I wore at weekends. She said, 'Percy, I think its time you *had a talk* with that boy.'

I suspect that I had been taking a more benign view of girls, in fact *any* view of girls, and from all angles which meant that I was starting to think about 'it'.

Kings Quay Creek, Isle of Wight. Two wildfowlers used to lie in wait for wild geese, chilled to the bone, purple noses etc (men not geese). My father, bird-watcher, used to lie in wait with an oil drum and a stick: boom, boom, boom. 'Just one more time squire,' they told him, bloody furious, 'and you get your drumstick rammed so far up you won't get your cap on, right?'

So father took me for The Walk. At twelve and hardly surprisingly, I already knew what 'it' was about from school. Not sex education which was still in the very distant future (and it's-nothing-to-snigger-about-boy), but the lore of the outside lavs, which gave it to you straight, albeit inaccurately.

It seemed from what father was humming and hawing about that it was all about eggs – which it would have to be seeing as he was an amateur ornithologist. Male birds and mother birds. He was careful to avoid the word 'cocks'. He said that I had begun as an egg which was unsettling for a growing lad to think about because being 'daft as a brush', as they say in Yorkshire, I immediately visualised myself as a sort of Humpty Dumpty sitting on a wall and with a limited future. We were walking through this copse at the time.

'And where the hell do you think you're going?' this man said, springing out from behind a bush. He had a dog which drew back its upper lip in a sort if sneer, leather gaiters (the man) and a shotgun.

Father did his innocence act. He was not a good actor being of the Mary Pickford era. Silent movies, five minutes bodice-ripping and faces working convulsively, then the caption says, economically 'Never, never!'

The upshot was that we were trespassing and sent packing, leaving me with uneasy doubts. They'd said nothing about eggs behind the outdoor lavs. How had mother coped with an egg that size? Phew! Father, thankful for the interruption, took us home along a different route altogether.

We ate our sandwiches by the river after he'd had his dip. Sometimes, in winter, he'd let me break the ice for him, which I did with the greatest of pleasure. 'Gawww. Ahhhhh!' he'd cry in a piping voice. 'Brrrrr!' He was totally bananas.

He found some owl vomit which he dissected for my education while I sat with jaws frozen on a fish-paste sandwich.

'Look, look!' he exclaimed, poking around with a bit of stick, 'Unless I'm much mistaken this is the beak of a meadow-pippit!' He held it up for my closer inspection. I gagged.

There was a film currently showing called *Sanders of the River* about Zulus and such. I cut some elderberry canes to use as assegais. We started crossing a field. I was M'boko, a Zulu warrior, 'Ulla-ulla-ulla!' I hollered, running on ahead, hurling my assegais. Suddenly father came tearing up astern, arms and legs pumping, binoculars and specimen box swinging.

'Bul-bul-bul!' he panted, plainly although atypically joining in the fun.

Well, I thought, 'Bul-bul' must be a Zulu war-cry, you would wouldn't you? Unusual behaviour for him, but then who was I to complain, it was better than eggs. I took off after him.

'Whahoo!' I yelled, slapping my own bum for extra speed, prancing in a spirited fashion.

There was this gate. Father went over it and I'll swear he never touched the top rail.

From behind me came a bellow and a thunder of hooves. There was this bloody great bull. I went over the gate like a collapsing deckchair.

Years later, I heard of a similar incident. 'Why,' said the farmer when challenged, 'that old bull wouldn't have hurt 'ee. Just wanted a bit of a game!'

Bath Time
Lads on the lookout for a boat can't afford to be fussy

U p to the age of twelve I lived in the centre of Yorkshire, remote from the sea and boats; unless one counted the river skiffs, hireable at an exorbitant sum per half hour and therefore beyond reach at fourpence a week pocket money.

I was only afloat in one once, as a treat, sitting rigidly upright as instructed to maintain equilibrium, father rowing, hogging the oars, beating the water to froth. There was a rudder with a yoke and two lines which was mother's job, and which brought upon her head a non-stop haranguing to pull whichever line father deemed necessary to keep us in mid-stream. Other skiffs passed in either direction, each with its wind-milling oarsman and bedevilled steersman – or woman, tight of lip and ominous. A fine treat that was. I needed a boat of my own and to hell with hire skiffs.

Opportunity was about to blossom. From our living room, and beyond our back garden fence, you could see this row of agricultural cottages whose tenants were what mother called 'common-as-muck!' Which was not what you might have called a particularly refined description, but there you are.

The women had muscles like Popeye and their kids were robust but knickerless, constantly the target of verbal abuse in broad Yorkshire, 'Wipe tha mucky snout our Maureen!' The fathers were seen only on Sundays, after milking and mucking out, large, leather-belted men in flat caps who were best avoided.

Outside each cottage and facing us stood the brick privies where the grandads sat with their keks round their ankles, reading their sports pages and as mother said, 'Oh *very nice*, I must say!' What interested me and my mates, though, was what hung on a nail on the wall alongside each privy door: tin baths.

Come Friday nights, these galvanized tin baths would be taken indoors, stood in front of the kitchen range, filled with hot water from the copper nearby and the family, beginning with father, would take its weekly bath. The water, presumably, becoming progressively, dynastically, fouler by the time the smallest brat took its turn.

It seemed to me an excellent arrangement. Our bathroom was refrigerated, an iron bath stood on cast-iron claws which clutched cast-iron balls as though about to fire a broadside. A gas-geyser ominously named 'The Vesuvius' in curly letters boomed into play with a fall-out of fine ash.

My mate, Dicky Bray, was the first to spot the maritime potentials of a tin bath.

'Ay up,' he said, 'you could use one of them for a boat!'

The idea was born but how were we to give it substance? Plainly we couldn't just nick one – the size of the men and the muscles of their wives precluded this, besides which I had to go to confession on Saturday nights. 'Pray father I have sinned. I have nicked this tin bath...!' Catholicism, according to mother, was a great comfort to her. But then she wasn't nicking tin baths.

Then we remembered The Tip. Our personal wonderland, the huge hole in the ground into which people chucked things. It was not a rubbish tip for kitchen waste and nasty stuff; you could find pram wheels and discarded crutches, an enema syringe in its tin box, World War I gas masks and bedsteads, lavatory lids and if lucky we'd find, somewhere, a tin bath. I took the enema syringe home, and blasted the cat until grandad told me what it was for. We put on the gas masks and grunting and snorting, scared the living daylights out of two old ladies who thought we were dying.

At last we found it. Tin baths were about four feet in length, with handles. Ours was heavily overgrown with nettles and there was a hole in it. Beetles scuttled and large pink worms squirmed. It was as good as new.

We repaired the rusty hole by the canvas and paint technique, the paint found on site and an old school satchel providing the canvas. 'Good as new!' said Dicky, 'tha'd never know't difference!'

We loaded our bath onto my trolley and headed for water, which happened to be a flooded field.

We launched it, I clambered in and it fell over. Both wellies full. The water was a foot deep. Dicky had a go and by sitting low down and motionless, elbows in, eyes straight ahead and talking out of the corner of his mouth he proved that short voyages were possible. When he got out he also proved that paint-and-canvas patches also work on trouser seats.

We made a double paddle by sacrificing two ping-pong bats and a broomstick, and all the following weekend was spent splashing to and fro. But wider horizons beckoned and the river Ure in particular, a field away.

It had its origin in the Dales and it was fast and deep, given to flash flooding and with a dismal mortality rate. It was the sort of river that gives the guardian angels, charged with guarding young lads, peptic ulcers, and makes them indulge in compulsive feather-plucking.

The week passed slowly. We had left our 'boat' moored to a hedge so it should have been safe. We decided that we would have to pull it over the grass to a point well upstream, and float down to a shallow bit. We couldn't wait to become statistics. We were as daft as a rubber corkscrew.

Saturday morning. Booted, to ensure that we would really sink, we clumped along to the field, climbed the gate and were brought up with a round turn as they say, whoever 'they' might be. We stood and gaped, outrage lighting up our ear lobes a fiery red. We spluttered, we cried out in frustration and anger...

There stood our pride on four bricks. Not only on four bricks, but with a hosepipe trickling into it. There was this horse, it took a long, slurping gulp, lifted its dripping moustache, looked at us and farted.

The Running Moor
A lesson in seamanship and bare-faced cheek

Once a fanatical boatowner finds that a lad shares his obsession, it is like being taken over by a naturist, get-em-off time, deep breaths and 'who's for rounders?' You are accepted and committed. Invitations follow.

He said, 'Be at Sunbeam Yard, nine o'clock sharp to catch the ebb'. Well a ball and chain couldn't have stopped me. The yacht was a gaff cutter with chain nips and baggywrinkles everywhere, like some sort of hairy parasitical growth to be sprayed with Paraquat. We were under way right on the dot and we poled out into the river because there wasn't a breath of wind. With our sails hanging in droopy bights, we floated among the dead crabs, dud light bulbs and other harbour detritus all going down-river on the ebb.

The owner, I discovered, was a do-it-under-sail man. Nowadays, with yacht marinas divided up like egg boxes his kind are the bane of Harbour Masters and ferry skippers whose hands are never off the whistle. We had a great fat, green Kelvin down below, but it got as much use as a corkscrew at a temperance hotel.

The strengthening ebb carried us, mainly beam-on, seaward. We fended off buoys and other moored yachts whose owners, waving boathooks, wished us God-speed, and offered us advice much of which was anatomical and impossible. I stored it away for future use because this is how you learn.

It was a day spiced with lore and traditional skills. We scandalised our mizzen, rucked our nock, executed a Gravesend luff, hove-to for lunch and drudged stern-first down past the Bramble Bank in company with a bellowing P & O liner. It was a day of rich experience destined to become richer yet.

'How would you like to try a running moor lad?' he asked, knowing full-well what my answer would be, and that I hadn't the faintest bloody idea what he was talking about. There was this particular creek that was ideal for it.

'We'll bring up on a tight moor fore-and-aft,' he said. 'There ain't much water, but we'll have it all to ourselves!' Which is the sort of prediction you should shun like the Black Death.

On the way up-creek he explained my duties to me. I must let go the bower, run it out full scope, bang her in, then let go my kedge and middle on both. He added, 'Timing lad, it's timing and a cool head!' A cool cheek would have expressed it better.

I was on the fo'c's'le sorting my marbles. We came sweeping round this bend, fair tide and following wind and there was this one little yacht anchored slap in the middle of the fairway.

'Let go the bower!' came the awaited order.

I jerked the brake off and away she went with a mighty splash followed by the roar of chain, first the clean and shiny stuff then the rusty grot, the dog-ends, fluff, fly buttons and crab's legs.

'Check!' he hollered. I banged the brake on; the cable rose juddering and we began to swing. Round swept our stern like a battle-axe then BANG, alongside the little yacht...

The hatch flew back and the owner came rocketting up as though fired from a cannon. I watched in awe. He opened his gob in preparation for a blast but my skipper beat him to it.

'What a bloody stupid place to anchor!' he howled.

It was a valuable lesson. *The other man apologised.*

6

Never Mind Yer Bow Wave
Getting to windward is what matters

A bad boat makes a good teacher and if she won't tack, goes to windward like a cardboard box and generally behaves like a nun in a gale, she'll improve your seamanship no end.

We had named her *Nighthawk*, this having a rake-hellish ring to it, but I should have consulted father's bird books first. Nighthawk, it seemed was another name for the peaceable nightjar, also known as the 'fern-owl' or 'goat-sucker' which is a regrettable name for a sea-going vessel.

She was a fourteen-foot fisherman's skiff (the boat was fourteen foot not the fisherman) and in need of many improvements not least to her windward qualities which were virtually nil, and had already been the cause of our being rescued and towed into Portsmouth at the dead of night.

Despite pigs of iron ballast and two sacks of sand, she made fearsome leeway, leaving a great fan of a wake. You'd have the helm hard up, the rudder would be boiling with turbulence and you'd get an impression of speed without actually going anywhere except to leeward. The only way to tack her was by sticking a sweep out aft and flailing.

Les, our fisherman mentor, had much to say on the matter, mainly in the form of aphorisms, accompanied by much wagging of the head. 'Never mind yer bow wave, watch yer wake,' he'd say. 'It ain't where she *looks* its where she *goes* what matters... don't go sailin' ter loo'rd before you can git her to wind'rd.' When we tried to sit her out rather than taking a tuck of reef down he waxed wrath. 'If she's half out of water she's only half under bleedin' control!' He wasn't keen on windward sailing though. 'Gennelum don't go ter wind'rd unless they's racing. Only fools and fishermen goes ter wind'rd deliberate and fishermen don't get no bleedin' choice!'

It needed a second misadventure before we took heed of Les's advice. Ryde Middle Bank was only a couple of miles from Wootton

15

Creek, but due to the prevailing sou'westerly they were leeward miles. In the proper season you could hook whiting by the bucketful. Whiting taste of blotting paper but they are considered nourishing for invalids. Undaunted by not knowing any lucky invalids to benefit from this bonanza, and profusion making up for lack of flavour, we went after them hell-bent and downwind.

We anchored with twenty fathoms of Woolworth's clothesline on the tail of the bank, impaled our lugworms and got fishing. First came the drizzle, then the strengthening wind. We began to roll and plunge in a rising sea, whiting and invalids forgotten as we snatched and jerked at our anchor line, which was looking thinner by the moment.

It was around noon. We were getting scared, but it was all too plain that we must not attempt to lift our anchor – we had that much sense. There was no way we would be able to flog back up-wind. In any case, we hadn't the weight to sit her out, and she had the weatherly qualities of a fat man carrying a ladder. It was a long and scary afternoon spent huddled under the gunn'le; cold and wet, visibility almost nil.

It was early evening before the front passed, the wind eased and we attempted a half-rowing, half-sailing claw back to the shelter of the land. We had acquired four whiting and a wealth of new wisdom. We were resolved to do something about that lack of weatherliness.

We could do nothing about our sails which consisted of an old red jib from a larger boat which had been in use as somebody's boat-cover, and which we'd nicked. We set it as a gunter-mainsail with a bamboo curtain-pole gaff. Our headsail(s) were my scout tent opened out flat and cut diagonally corner-to-corner. Having two identical jibs meant that we had to rig a bowsprit. They set atrociously but looked shippy. We decided to put a daggerboard in her.

This meant cutting a slot in a garboard strake alongside the keel and building a case inside the boat down through which a plank or 'dagger' could be thrust and thereby provide 'lateral resistance'. This was a technical term which we rolled around our tongues like connoisseurs sampling a new and exciting vintage. The case leaked prodigiously. We dismantled it and re-bedded it on a fat wodge of that panacea of leaks in old wooden boats, tar-and-cement. Fat black worms of the stuff oozed out from every joint and we knew we had won. The trouble was, however, that we had made the case too wide and since you had to sit on it while rowing, the slightest wave sent a jet of water straight up your bum.

Fired by enthusiasm we added foredeck, side decks and coamings, also bottom-boards and an invention of mine intended to give warning of impending capsize which I named the Angleometer. The bottom part of a Cherry Blossom shoe polish tin was fixed amidships. It had a pendulum and red-painted sectors.

'Just keep one eye on it and you can't go wrong!' I forecast falsely to my doubting mate 'Spoofer' Murray. 'Once your pendulum gets into the red, ease sheets and luff her!'

Ingenious though it might have been, it was bloody useless in practice since the pendulum oscillated dizzily and you ended up pumping the tiller, perched up on the gunn'le like a boy camel-jockey.

There came a day when we were dropping down the Medina through Cowes, no wind, me standing up pushing the sweeps, Spoofer steering and giving unheeded pilotage information. We had to pass the Royal Yacht Squadron, which is the equivalent of sinners passing the Pearly Gates.

'Smarten up. Let's see a bit of swank!' I told Spoof.

It was the signal for a puff of wind; our sails filled, we heeled and I shipped my oars. In doing so I committed an arch-crime of seamanship: I left the blades stuck out ahead like a pair of bunny ears. As we heeled over, in went the leeward blade and acting like a submarine's diving

17

plane, over she went. We cast off everything in sight, scrambled up to windward and she came back down with a mighty wallop. We drifted past the Squadron half-awash, sails flogging and bailing frenetically.

Then came the matter of mother's lodger, 'Papa'. We called him that behind his back, the creep. After all our striving to make the boat more efficient, he had to stick his beak in didn't he!

He was a pert little man with a dicky bow tie and goatee beard like that Colonel who advertises fried chicken. At the breakfast table he had to sit on two cushions, perched up like a tennis referee and he always had *two* boiled eggs to our one. He was fussy about how they were done. He would prod and poke with his spoon and you'd see mother's lips getting tighter. 'Nearly right!' the little bastard would say, prodding away, 'never mind though, I'll manage to eat it!' He was easy to loathe, he knew all about everything including boats – he said so.

One day he had watched me fitting a tar-tingle on the boat, which as everybody knows is a bit of tarry canvas placed over a crack and held down by a bit of sheet lead and copper tacks. It didn't meet with his approval, and he said so the next day at breakfast.

'The last thing I want to do "mother",' he always addressed her thus when I was the object of his attentions, 'the very last thing I want to do, is appear a spoilsport but it has to be said. I don't think that Desmond's boat repairs are good enough!'

And so of course my father was urged by mother to look it over, even though he knew as much about boat repairs as a Naga tribesman knows about church embroidery.

Luckily, he had had just one trip in the boat. It was when I took him out to see the redshanks, or 'reb-shanffs' as he called them once his teeth were in his pocket. In fact what he said was 'fuff the red-shanffs!' Accordingly, having looked at my tar-tingle the matter went no further.

At the time, we were living in the old converted coach house of Binstead Hall, a Victorian ostentation, that was empty but with its own boathouse which we used, nobody having said we shouldn't. The boat was on rollers ready to launch. There was a big spring tide that day and she was almost afloat, just needing one shove.

What you couldn't see was the step or cill just by the door, it being under water. The boat was half in the boathouse. Papa arrived in his little gum-boots and pork-pie hat.

'I see I'm just in time lads!' he cried, taking over command unasked. 'I'll take the weight at the back until you're ready to push.' We didn't mention to him that there was *no need* to push, she was half afloat on her rollers.

'Right, I've got her!' he cried, heaving and disappearing, sitting down in two feet of water.

The Legacy
A bargain I couldn't refuse

I've got a hunch I'll need a packed lunch –
It isn't easy to guess –
For although I may go
To Tierra del Fuego,
It's more likely to be Skegness.

Hungry for nautical knowledge I joined the Sea Scouts. We had this varnished six-oar gig, glossy as a grand piano but not glossy enough for our Scout Master. He put a bottle in a bag and clouted it with a hammer.

'Scrapers,' he explained succinctly, handing out lethal shards. We scraped her down to bare wood, bleeding generously despite holding these wicked fragments of glass in bits of newspaper. Then we varnished her ten coats achieving mirror perfection, and teaching us that boats have to be cosseted and looked after if they are to look after us.

That was how you learned about boats in the pre-World War II era, the hard way, kneeling at the feet of the experts and lapping up wisdom. You took a gamble that you wouldn't be taught rubbish though. It was the classic Boyhood of Raleigh situation, pink-cheeked tyros sitting cross-legged at the feet of an elder who might well have been teaching them utter crap.

But you learned good habits like stowing oars in a boat blades-forward, coiling everything in sight instinctively, which was tough on snakes, keeping fenders out of the water and stowing sails with pride. There were no sailing schools and no evening classes in navigation where long-retired Commanders RN bored you witless with Var and Dev, enlivened only by having forgotten to do their flies up, poor old souls.

Our general mentor was fisherman, Les, whose wife's clothesline was rigged with varnished blocks that he'd nicked and best yacht manila, spliced, parcelled and served, which had left a neglected cruiser the poorer by a jib halliard. He knew everything. My *personal* mentor, however, was my mate, 'Spoofer's' grandad.

He owned a fourteen-foot half-deck day-boat. Spoof avoided sailing with him. He knew to his cost that to do so meant being treated with the full military discipline reserved for grandsons. The old man had been a military policeman in Malaya. He treated all novices as half-wits, addressing them loudly and slowly, on the assumption that the most complicated technicality became clear if shouted loudly enough.

'Trice up your tack!' he would bellow, enunciating deafeningly, or 'Reeve your reef pennant man!' either command being enough to reduce the hapless tyro to fumbling humiliation.

His boat, *Daphne,* was typical of the pre-war dayboat, many of which were local One-designs which still survive. They were built and raced with dedication; heavy with massive steel or gunmetal centreplates, and intended to be sailed upright. Capsizes were (and are) rare and attended, when they occur by considerable fuss and commotion, unlike the modern dinghy sailor who has been known to capsize in order to have a quick pee, righting it with a flip of the buttocks.

Daphne, typically, was a little ship in her own right and equipped generously with bucket and bailer, sponge and squeegee, boathook, jib-stick, boxed compass, Vim, Brasso, shammy leathers, touch-up paint and varnish, cushions, fenders, oars, spare tiller, anchor and cable, warps, hand-lead, bosun's bag, burgee, ensign and staff.

Beneath each side deck there were tiny lockers to contain these items, each in its own place, and should the Vim be found with the hand-lead instead of Brasso, it was as shocking a misdemeanour as finding the young master's pants in the maid's bedroom.

The boat had to be scrubbed meticulously after every sail and her cotton sails dried and furled like city umbrellas, the pipe-clayed covers laced on exactly right. Being on a mooring involved a dinghy tender and more fuss, for dinghy and half-decker *must never be allowed to touch* and the dinghy rowlocks must be unshipped, oars inboard and fenders out before even getting alongside.

The owner in his cap and reefer, would finally give the order to 'Cast off forr'd', and a whole new chapter of ritual and correct seamanship would begin plus a host of orders delivered ringingly, and in compliance with nautical procedure and etiquette. That boat never seemed to heel or chuck spray about and the old gent would sit at the tiller bolt upright, like one of those little tin men in clockwork toy motor cars, ruddy-cheeked and one-dimensional. Sadly, all this was destined to change and I was to change it.

One day he said, 'I'm going to give up sailing and I'd like you to buy this boat from me Desmond.'

He might just as well have been offering to sell me Tower Bridge – a once-only offer, tell you what I'll do, I'll chuck in Westminster Bridge and Big Ben. I was deeply embarrassed. How could I reveal my shallow pocket?

'I, er, well ah...' I mumbled.

The old gent might not have heard me. 'I've got the bill of sale here,' he said, producing it, complete with twopenny stamp to make it legal. It sold me everything for one shilling. I was speechless, scarlet, stammering.

He never even smiled. Precise and pernickity that he was, he loved that little boat. Rather than sell her he *gave her to me*. It was like finding a good home for a beloved old gun dog.

In the years that followed I tried my hardest to maintain the boat as he had done, to sail her with equal care but I was seventeen and she sailed on her beam ends, chucked water around, got muddy and ran aground, but I tried, I really did try.

When I went into the army, rather than leave her to bleach and get filled with leaves lying unused and unwanted, and since I could not sell her but must hand her on in trust, I gave her to a Scout Troop in Cowes who wrecked her by neglect in a single year.

Courting Jane
Goats and warm evenings are a poor combination

Courtship used to be a lengthy business. It was like queueing in the Post Office, ten minutes shuffling along foot at a time, wrong window! There was a lot of eye-balling done. I'd be going to work on my bike and Jane would be on the bus, same seat, staring straight ahead, eyes right while I sat at the lane end waiting for the bus to pass.

Me on a mare called Ladybird. *She taught me to jump. Every time I bent over to tighten her girth she bit my arse.*

Actually I'd time it like a military operation with zeroed watches, leaving home at *exactly* 0735. I'd wear my laconic Clark Gable expression with the lifted eyebrow. We never smiled at one another or exchanged the faintest sign of recognition. She was very pretty, although for a year I only saw her head, then we came face-to-face walking. She was of short stature, well-endowed. Come off it mate, she was fat.

Dinner-hour walks. She was pig-ignorant when it came to boats and I was to get her afloat only once when she sat square, knees together, bloody great handbag on lap, while I darted around her trying to handle mainsheet, tiller and jib without becoming too familiar, seeing it was early stages.

Meanwhile the walks. Like many fat girls she aspired to being kittenish and expected to be lifted over stiles which was like trying to grapple with a fridge-freezer. You can't get a proper grip. Grunting with effort, features twisted by the hellish strain, I would get her up as far as the top bar where I would lodge her temporarily. 'Hang on,' I'd say, 'while I get a proper purchase' – to which she seemed to take umbrage.

Inevitably there came the time when I asked her to come to the pictures with me, which in the custom of the time meant 'how about a grope?' She agreed. I had tried it on with no success while dinner-hour walking but she had said, 'None of that!' and hand-bagged me. She said that our friendship was platonic but I'll bet you that Plato tried it on at the pictures.

Saturday evening, best kit, Brylcreem, a dab under the armpits and here I come. What's showing? Who cares. It was a warm evening, a very warm evening. I was just getting my bike out when our neighbour's goat got loose. 'Have you got a minute?' he asked, well aware that I had.

He had two nannies and a billy, who was like a rug on legs, and who could perform the remarkable feat of peeing in his own face, a despicable show-off of course and ignored by the nannies, but it shows you the sort of unprincipled bastard he was.

'You get round behind him and grab his horns,' my neighbour said, arms extended, advancing purposefully. The billy turned its head and fixed me with a yellow eye. 'Heheheh,' it said.

'Steady boy,' I said and grabbed for its horns. It was like a motor bike scramble. I should have worn a helmet and goggles. Dirt and hot cinders flying, neighbour flapping his bloody arms, me grappling, goat peeing. Oh it was a joy to watch, I'm sure.

Afterwards the neighbour, grateful, brushed me down because I was covered in goat. 'I won't forget this!' he said, truthfully enough. I sure as hell wouldn't either!

Being a warm evening meant that inside the cinema, despite the ventilators and extractors blasting away, it was very hot indeed. Down went the lights, Pathé News followed by Donald Duck and choc-ices. Very hot it was. I got my arm round. Big picture came on. Buttons! Jane started sniffing. Everybody else was sniffing, then I started sniffing, and the stink got worse.

'What's that horrible smell?' Jane hissed. Then she drew back in disgust. '*Why it's YOU!*' she proclaimed.

At which point she rose to her feet and made for the exit, leaving me at the centre of a ring of hostile, sniffing faces. Brylcreem and underarm care don't stand a hope in hell against hot eau de billy goat.

The Passing of Paddy
It was an undignified way to go, but strangely in character

I have pondered on how best to handle this delicate subject. Should I edge around it on tiptoe, like negotiating a muddy doorway, or should I plough straight in with both feet? Since I get covered in it either way though, why mince matters?

It is this; men have been peeing over the side in boats for as long as boats have had sterns and men have had a need. I must air the matter because it cost us old Paddy, a good friend.

Why do we do it? Is it laddish vulgarity, an urge to offend against the social niceties or is it more of a comfortable male bonding exercise? Anyway, why bumble and bang around down below in a space like a bedroom wardrobe when we can stand elbow-to-elbow and stare at the stars?

We don't do it where it causes offence, or in marinas unless it is very, very late at night and the beer has been abundant. Neither do we line the after-deck in places like the Suffolk marshes, where the marron grass rustles in the night breeze and the beam of Orford lighthouse sweeps the anchorage once every six seconds.

Paddy – and if he had a second name we never knew it – was a loner, an ex-tank driver from the Western desert, a lugubrious-looking man with a droopy moustache, a cockeyed grin and that self-deprecating Irish humour. His home was a converted decked-in ex-naval Montague whaler, which was like living in a drainpipe. It was currently berthed in Southampton where he had a job of sorts in a factory.

One day he went to work as usual and suddenly he thought, 'I pull this bloody handle twice every minute and that is all I have to do. It has taken me a million years to achieve my present state of evolution. There has to be more to life than this!' So he chucked in his job, collected his money and cards and just left. The foreman watched him peddle off on his bike. You never knew with Irishmen.

It was early in March and the wind blew cold and bleak, force five to six from the nor-west and an early dusk had brought night too soon. Paddy tied two reefs down and headed down Southampton Water, bound for Wootton Creek on the Isle of Wight where we, his mates, were. Even loners can get lonely.

Meanwhile, Murray and I aboard this Looe lugger were getting ready to turn in. The bogey-stove was dying down, pinging and creaking as the cast iron cooled. We had been on deck and pee'd over the lee rail, tapped our pipes out, put them with our baccy pouches and matches in our caps in proper sailing fashion. In an emergency we could be capped, flashed-up and puffing in an instant.

There came a great commotion on deck and the hatch was thrown open. The fug we had achieved below went up into the bitter night like a great bat. 'Hey, shut it, shut it!' we chorused. Then we saw that it was Paddy. He just stood there swaying and grinning his crooked grin. He was soaked to the skin and shaking with cold. He said, 'Boys, I've lost me all!'

He would *have* to say that! Not 'I've lost everything!' or 'lost the lot', but *'lost me all!'* Then we realised that he was drunk, sober-drunk, on the verge of collapse. We stripped him, towelled him, stoked the bogey-stove until the 'charley noble' on deck was belting a stream of red sparks, wrapped him in blankets and poured scalding Bovril down him.

'Sweet mither o' God will you boggers let up now!' he choked, a Bovril fountain and in need of air. He began, falteringly and half asleep, to tell us the story.

With everything he possessed, including his bike, aboard the whaler the passage had been fast and hard. His tiller-arm had ached with the strain of a strong quartering wind, and the waves running alongside were like hunting dogs, leaping and snapping. The open stretch beyond Calshot and the dangerous tumble off Bramble Bank were almost too much for him to handle. Then they were under the land off the island and sailing fast along the shore; Wootton was a mile ahead to starboard.

As the mouth of the creek opened up, he met the full weight of the wind funnelling down it. He could either reach for the marked channel and come hard on the wind, or he could short-cut across the shallows inside Wootton Rocks and get into the shelter of the bend of the creek. He had a chart but it was down below and the helm could not be left. Also he was a stubborn, pig-headed, 'sure-what's-the-problem?' bloody-minded Irishman.

The whaler hit the rocks full-on, rose from the water, rolled on her beam, lifted again and descended with a rending crash that broke her in half like a stick.

Paddy, breathless from the chill, began floundering shorewards. Weighed down by his duffle coat, his boots too tight to be kicked off, he flogged and floundered blindly. Kept going, because he was a bloody-minded Pat. Kept on just flailing until a wave flung him up the beach.

There was a lane to the village and Paddy, weaving like a drunk, followed it to the pub. He said nothing, just bought the Scotch, found a corner, drank it, puked and then they threw him out.

Somebody said, 'I hate to see a man in that condition, revolting!' So they chucked him out, which was when he went in search of his mates, as he should have done in the first bloody place.

We left him to sleep it off. We got the dinghy launched. The tide was high and so was half a moon. It was playing 'stop-thief' with the black tatters of racing cloud as we pulled tandem down-creek to Wootton Point and beached the boat, and hoofed it over the spit to where Paddy had come ashore.

It looked like half a side of beef with ribs curving, but it was half a boat and:

Half a chart, a shirt, a boot, a varnish brush, a can of fruit. Books and beans and sails and socks, love letters in a chocolate box...

The rest of Paddy's possessions, his 'all', were spread the length of the beach and we mustered friends next day, with sacks in a mournful treasure hunt. Meanwhile we pulled back up-creek with what little we had salvaged.

We found Paddy sitting up. He had found paper and pencil. He was sketching a whaler, a successor.

'What d'you reckon boys; I'll increase deck camber and shorten the cockpit, would-yez look at that now!' Which we duly did and made approving noises and Paddy, well-pleased, fell asleep as if we'd slugged him.

Paddy had a great many friends and no enemies. There was a whip-round. We kitted him out from corn-pad to toothbrush, from army great-coat to underpants and a kit-bag to put it in. The silly old sod went and wept on us, which was what western desert tank drivers with burn scars aren't supposed to do, and we felt humbled and said 'Aw shit!' and kicked stones.

Nemesis had her hooks into Paddy.

A couple of weeks later, because he was an adventurer, he joined a gang of lads who had the idiotic idea of sailing an ancient, long, narrow-gutted, ex-Lord-knows-what inland racing boat across to Cherbourg for a boozy weekend. It seemed like a good idea to Paddy.

Afterwards they didn't want to talk about it. We could guess the details anyway. Paddy was on watch, the rest were below at breakfast – it was a raw, bleak morning, mid-Channel, whole mainsail, going like a hooked salmon.

Through the hatch they saw him go. He was having a pee. No cry, just *gone*. I'll bet he was joking. I'll bet he was saying something ribald about hoisting a signal or passing a towrope or something of the sort because he was Paddy.

Of course they tried everything, every manoeuvre; round and round, tack, gybe, much hurling of rope's ends, hang on, hang on.

They said, guiltily, that at the end he looked *almost comic*, with his drooping moustache, like a walrus. Boots, army greatcoat? Not a chance! They went round once more and he wasn't there. No great fuss, just not there any more.

Paddy left us a lesson. Your bare hand cannot grip a guardrail wire with the full weight of your falling body upon it.

Don't try grabbing the rail at sea... Don't pee over the side.

A Sour Gift

A genuine Brixham trawler of my very own

Lying at anchor in Falmouth was this ex-Breton tunnyman. She'd been brought over by escaping fishermen one jump ahead of the jackboots early in the war.

She was unmistakably a sailing tunnyman, although her great rods had been taken off her. The long, raking counter stern was the clue – the raking stern that had sunk half a fleet while hove-to in north Biscay, hobby-horsing, slapping that long tail down, shaking them to pieces.

I had once been privileged to watch one of the last of the sailing tunnymen entering the harbour at Ile de Groix. In a thunderstorm. There was a jagged flash of lightning and there she was framed in the entrance like a great moth against a windowpane, wings spread, her twin rods like antennae.

From the ensuing darkness came a great squealing of blocks, thumps, heavy thuds. The lightning flashed again half a minute later, and I saw that she had all sail off her, carrying her way – for she was engineless – to crash alongside. How had those sails come down so fast, chain luffs and railway line lashed to her gaffs? Her crew wore berets and designer-stubble. They looked at our prissy yacht topsides, scantily protected by their motor tyres and said 'Pouf' in a disdainful fashion.

I was leaning on the seawall watching when the owners strolled by. They invited me aboard and we chatted. They were brothers, a couple of 'Brummy' ex-owners of a garage who, with wives and kids, planned to emigrate to South Africa in the tunnyman. I asked, 'Why South Africa? Everybody was going to Australia.'

'Owstralia was too far. Yow can follow the cowst to South Africa!'

I hoped he was joking. There was a lot of communal jollity, but in the eyes of their wives there was a secret corner of fear poorly disguised, like a stain on a carpet hidden by moving furniture, but you don't leave coffee tables in doorways.

I had arrived in Falmouth on a yacht delivery and I was due to catch a train back to Chichester next morning. I spent the evening in a water-front pub, which was how I came to meet one of the brothers again. We talked. I gave him the benefit of my deep-sea experience which was nil and courtesy of the writings of Voss, Slocum and Claude Worth. I discussed the merits of streaming warps and using oil-bags. My personal experience of oil, bagged or loose, was limited to the Cod Liver Oil variety, malted and efficacious with growing boys; but he listened carefully and then treated me to an endless dissertation on cam-shafts and cartridge-starting procedures. We brimmed with beer and bonhomie. He had an auntie who kept alpaca goats.

The evening passed pleasantly; round followed round; things got knocked over. Between us we righted the national economy and pondered God. We reached the 'Ole pal' stage, the booze-and-bathos stage of swapping baccy pouches, although we were both smoking the same brand. We were in fact both thoroughly pissed.

Last orders were being called and ashtrays were being emptied, chairs put on tables, subtle hints that it was time we all got the hell out of it. My companion and I stood nose-to-nose and swaying. We were out of synchronisation and conversation was not easy. He said, suddenly, having reached a decision.

'Aw well,' he said, ' I wanna wiss you all the besh,' he swayed one way and I swayed the other. We collided, supported one another. I wissed him all the besh also.

'I wanna let you have thish!' he concluded and handed me a piece of much-thumbed Basildon Bond. It was a bill of sale for the Brixham trawler, *Leonora Minnie*. They had bought her and transferred her engine to the tunnyman. She was lying in Langstone Harbour and might need a bit of work on her, but I was welcome to her.

We bid one another goodbye with the street lights swirling and whirling about our swaying heads, and with a seemingly interminable handshake that was more a matter of mutual support than a gesture of friendship. We tacked off down the street in our separate directions. I never knew what became of them. But then Falmouth is a place of farewells, of youths with chin-fringe beards and guitars, off to find the rainbow and ending up broke in Gibraltar, of communes and 'getting away from it all'. They left and never came back.

Later, when I studied the document I found that it had been countersigned to 'The Bearer'. As a legal document; and despite its tuppenny stamp, I had uneasy doubts, but I was determined to put its validity to the test.

I travelled back next day in a state of euphoria. Engineless she might be; needing a bit of work done, no problem. I would sail her away and I would fit her out and start chartering. I sat up straighter, the new owner of the sailing trawler, *Leonora Minnie*, and Master Under God, who as yet had not been told.

Langstone Harbour near Portsmouth is one of those vast knee-deep stretches where boats are either aground, about to run aground or their owners are straining their guts to get them off a mud-bank. A narrow track led me to the water's, or mud's edge, according to state of tide. There was no sign of a Harbour Master's office nor sign of any vessel resembling a Brixham trawler. I would have to ask somebody.

There was a man with a bike and trouser-clips. He had a bait-digger's box and a fork wrapped in sacking. Gum-boots were lashed to his carrier; he was plainly a man who would know every boat in the harbour since he would dig holes all around them at low tide in his quest for ragworms.

'Excuse me,' I opened. 'I don't suppose you happen to know where the *Leonora Minnie* is moored do you?'

'The old *Minnie*? Yes, in a manner of speaking.' He was looking at me in an odd sort of smirky way. 'Dependin' on what you mean by *moored* squire.'

'Well, where she's lying.'

'Which is different, she's *lying* right there,' and he pointed. There was a mast decorated with banners of seaweed and a deckhouse covered in seagull shit, a row of stanchions awash.

'Ah!' I said.

'If you knows who owns her the 'arbour Master would be glad to know...'

'Yes,' I said very carefully, 'I'm quite sure that he would!' I turned and walked away in a gingerly fashion. I even managed to whistle a little tune to signify my total indifference. I just wanted to get the hell out.

To be a Skipper
I wasn't cut out to be her Ladyship's poodle

Jumbo fender, petite Brenda,
Forgotten all they taught her;
Silly bitch used the wrong hitch,
Guess who's in the water?

The skipper's role ranges from the big ship's Captain, who is God Almighty in a company cap and seen by yachtsmen as a pair of nostrils sixty feet up, to the skipper of the small family cruiser or 'dad' who has a status problem.

He also has to carry the dustbin down to the front gate on Tuesday nights and bath the dog after rolling in something. He answers the door when the Plymouth Brethren call. Despite this, he must assert his authority aboard for the safety of all. He tries it, 'For heaven's sake Wilfred stop that silly nonsense!' she says and that's that.

Then there is the charter yacht skipper. If he's lucky, he gets the mixed bag paying crew who can be blasted without pity for dropping peach stones down the loo; if he is unlucky, he gets the private charterer who treats him like garden furniture. Between the two types comes a vast permutation ranging from lovable old Ned, unsackable because of his bad back, and the Admiral's Cup Autocrat who weighs your pocket fluff before allowing you on board.

Barring him and big ships I have skippered them all, even to being a private motor cruiser skipper and expected to mow the lawn when not engaged in a maritime role. I lasted a week. The motor cruiser swung around her mooring unused and in full view of the house which was thatched with a thatched car-port, letter-box and bird-bath and a wishing well that went nowhere. I spurned the mower and got sacked.

'Sleightholme,' she said, 'I'm afraid we're going to have to let you go!' conjuring up visions of a lid being lifted, a flutter of wings and old Sleightholme soaring off up into the wide blue yonder, 'God-speed my little feathered friend!'

Thus it was that when the chance to skipper this ex-Lowestoft sailing trawler for a week – her regular skipper being laid up, practising for a bad back – came along, I grabbed it.

Her skipper, Frank, lived in East Cowes and I paid him a call in order to pick up a few tips. He wrote a character reference for me, it said; 'I have knowed the borer two year he is clean and sober.' It would have done for Dr Crippen, whom he didn't know either, but I wanted the job.

'Er course,' Frank said disparagingly, 'you being only a yachtie 'e'll want me back soonest!'

The yacht retained her gaff rig, but the authentic aura and aroma of unwashed flannel, shag tobacco and cod had long been supplanted by Lone Pine air freshener, Nivea cream and diesel.

She was lush as a bordello down below, kept that way by a steward called Walker or Watson, I forget, who was camp as a feather boa and had a fetish for tinned sardines. He said, 'Her Ladyship has the money, he's got the title right?'

She wore blue bell-bottoms and a blue gansey which combined to make her look like a sack of footballs. Sir Harold, by comparison was so unremarkable that he vanished before your eyes like back-bedroom wallpaper. Her Ladyship eyed me.

'Hmm,' she said, 'Sir Harold likes his hands in white overalls. You'll find some of the skipper's on a nail.'

At this stage, obedient and willing, I struggled into Frank's boiler suit and cap and returned on deck. I looked like an olde-time walk-on comic; I could have done with Dan Leno boots and a silly walk. The effort of hollowing my chest to accommodate the buttons left me with a curious gasping tone of voice. A button popped off. We looked at it. 'I think perhaps not!' she said, 'but you must try not to look like one of the guests,' I wondered which one.

The steward went ashore to do some last-minute shopping and flog the tins of sardines he'd been nicking. My Lady showed me her gum-boots. She said, 'Oh skipper, my boots need washing.'

'They do don't they,' I agreed affably, wandering off. None of those lawn-mower larks this time.

The guests included two poor relations in Woolworths sandshoes and two men in big caps with facial hair tufts who stood with their hands cupped behind their backs. Plainly, they were either ex-naval officers or ex-cinema commissionaires, but when addressed by them, I instinctively felt and resisted the urge to reply, 'Aye, aye sir' and point my chin in the air.

We got under way, which is to say Sir started the engine and said to me 'Oh skipper can we, um, untie...' with which the ex-RN couple, as though driven by clockwork, started dashing around issuing orders to each other in nasal tones. 'Let go aft... all gone forr'd!' accompanied by a feverish hauling and coiling of ropes. Not getting as much as a look in, I adopted an authoritative stance and frowned. Her ladyship tore up and down, footballs in mighty motion, collecting fenders.

Our destination was across-Channel to Deauville and the casino, Sir navigating, me on sails, her ladyship on everybody's nerves. There was little breeze and we drummed along under main and mizzen.

So we and her ladyship made coffee – which is to say she spooned out the instant and the poor relations handed it round. I sat on the rail and chatted. Her ladyship had a word with Sir who came over to me looking embarrassed.

He cleared his throat. 'Hum,' he said, 'We...er, I think you might be...it might be more *suitable* if you went forward and joined steward hum!'

So I joined Walker hum. When we'd collected up the empty mugs, her ladyship, to my huge surprise volunteered to wash up, which she did and, by some occult divination, washed all but two of them: Watford's and mine.

Harwich harbour entrance.
You may get took-short,
While entering the port,
This needn't overwhelm one;
You don't have to hurry or panic or worry,
Switch the Auto-helm on.

I blew it again on the matter of the staysail. The sunbathers took over the foredeck with her ladyship in prime position on the forehatch. In her stripy two-piece she looked like a middle ground buoy, two spheres, horizontal bars in red and white – pass either side. She had more spare tyres than Brands Hatch.

There came a fitful puff of breeze and I yanked the staysail aloft. 'No, no!' squeaked the creepy steward, 'you'll make a shadow on Madam!' Her ladyship, was already in full tongue.

Everybody was yelling, 'Get it down, get it down!' so I let it go at the run and it enveloped her!

The breeze was holding and not to be wasted. It was the work of a moment to get the jib on deck but I got no further.

'No,no, no,' Sir cried in triplicate, 'we never use THAT. It makes the deck leak!' Which wasn't surprising. The bowsprit bitts, twin posts piercing the deck and running below to connect with the keel, had been sawn off flush below-decks to make more room in the forecabin. The surprise was that *anybody* could be such a cloth-eared prat as to do such a thing. Wisely, I said nothing.

We berthed with a bit of a fuss, me on the wheel cutting the power as we ghosted alongside, Sir banging the throttle open again, then me having to bang her astern again. We tied up in heavy silence, nobody very happy. I had the feeling that I had cocked up my future, which I had.

Watkins or Watson and I were to stay aboard and eat sardines on toast while the party went ashore to dine and visit the casino. Her ladyship was painted up like a fairground horse and wearing a boat-cloak. She should have had opera hat, green eye-shadow and fangs, Count Dracula and back in her coffin by cockcrow. We turned in early.

It was gone 2am when the party returned, plus a couple they had met in the casino and who had to be given a tour of the ship and a nightcap. Count Dracula flung open the forecabin door.

'Crew's quarters,' she whispered deafeningly, 'Separate facilities, every comfort.' She should have added cat flap and sand tray.

We were destined for Brightlingsea in Essex; meanwhile we sailed, or rather motored on up-Channel to Boulogne where we spent a night in the basin for no clear reason that I could see. Next morning we left with a narrow escape from disaster. Sir was on the wheel, the ex-RN gents raced around giving technical cries and I coiled warps. I glanced forward. A cargo vessel was warping herself round preparatory to leaving also. She had a wire stretching right across the entrance!

'Seen the wire!' I shouted in Sir's ear.

'That's the horizon man!' her ladyship squawked.

'Then it's sagging in the bloody middle!' I snarled.

'What, what?' Sir cried, peering around myopically. I yanked the gear lever aft and seized the wheel from him, pumping it over hard. His knuckles sounded like an African xylophone. The wire loomed above our bows. I went hard astern which got us into all sorts of mess but missed the wire.

We left harbour in a heavy frost. Once clear of the entrance her ladyship gave me a good going-over... My attitude was 'most unsatisfactory!' she said, as though I was a piece of faulty equipment to be returned to the manufacturer with the till receipt. We would have to 'think seriously about our future relationship!' Too damn right we would.

I remained in deep ordure right across the Thames Estuary, down the Swin and into the River Coln and Brightlingsea, where I took a sounding and let go the anchor to ten fathoms (60 feet) on the hydraulic windlass.

Up came Sir and shortened it again to five. Her ladyship joined in and shortened it to almost up-and-down.

'But its only half-flood!' I spluttered.

'Don't we mean half-flood *sir*?' she said, footballs bouncing.

So I went below and packed my bag. In heavy silence I collected my pay, minus a tip, and the smirking steward put me ashore. I looked back at the yacht which was dragging nicely, nobody on deck. There was a boatman standing nearby.

'I'll nip out an' tell 'em. 'Arf a crown sir,' he said.

'Here's half a crown that says you don't!' I told him.

A Proper Little Palace
'Oops look at me rafters!' cried Robert,
goggling at the mess

Brenda, Brenda fetch a fender,
Hang it where you oughta;
Not over the bow, you silly cow,
Dangling in the water.

You get the golf club which owns its clubhouse, bar and course, around which the paying members stagger head-down against wind and rain in the pursuit of pleasure. Similarly you had the Island Cruising Club of Salcombe owning its boats for the use of members, the wind and the rain provided as part of the package.

What with a fleet of large cruising yachts as well as the shore-based dinghy section, there was a constant turnover of permanent staff, who were paid peanuts but fed, housed and provided with all the fresh air and nobility of purpose they could stomach. Naturally a job of this calibre attracted the nutters who were invited (warily) to come down on trial. Like the ex-Wren officer who aspired to become office manageress.

We billeted her overnight aboard *Hoshi* out on the mooring and, it being out of season, she had it all to herself. She wore huge navy-blue sandshoes like those little platforms which stop toy soldiers from falling over. She also wore a navy skirt and cardigan which flapped and flopped without any particular shape. She said she was looking forward to starting work.

'I used to have forty gels under me in "the Andrew",' she told us. We tried to visualise the grunting and cursing that might have ensued.

'Gels mean hanky-panky. Not under me though, no hanky-panky with my gels!' she said emphatically.

We were on spring tides and there was a fresh sou'westerly wind;

I once hung my sea-boot socks up to dry on the gallows behind my head. Somebody was sick in them. I skippered the Island Cruising Club's seventy-foot gaff schooner Hoshi *for nearly ten years off and on.*

twin phenomena which in Salcombe, when in opposition on an ebb tide meant that any vessel moored by its bow behaved like an unbroken stallion, tearing to and fro in a series of mad dashes, bringing up with a grinding crash of chain in fairlead, then with a howl of rigging, heeling steeply, and boring off in some new direction. The ebb was due to begin at around midnight on this particular occasion.

To us this was normal behaviour; you postponed supper for an hour or went ashore for an economical half-pint. It never occurred to me that a lady of such obvious maritime stamina might need to be warned.

Next morning when I went to pick her up she was on deck, bag packed, thin of lip and ominous as a grenade with the pin out. I gave her a cheery and experimental 'Good morning.'

'Not a wink!' she countered, 'Not one single wink of sleep have I had! Take me to the bus stop NOW!'

Which I did, without breakfast and winkless, single or double.

She was the first of a series of applicants for jobs, all a bit cuckoo, like Harry, who lasted until his past and a policeman caught up with him concerning a matter of embezzlement and bigamy. We all liked Harry.

He was followed by a complete prat – an indulged son of rich parents – with a pretty but faded wife and six kids. She looked as if she'd been too long in a shop window, rendered pale-ish and blue-ish, curling at the corners. He was engaged to drive the launch, a job he regarded as part of his personal plan for becoming a Trinity House Pilot, which he hoped to achieve by way of a correspondence course, once he could find one. He wrapped the launch around the landing pontoon and was sacked. Finally came Robert.

We needed a cook-housekeeper for the dinghy sailing section, and Robert, as an ex-ships' steward sounded promising. It was out of season and he would be aboard the Brixham trawler, *Provident*.

He arrived in a navy pilot jacket with a cheese-cutter cap perched on a tumble of curls. We went below. He took in the heavy deck-beams.

'Rafters!' he exclaimed in delight, clapping his hands, 'Ooo I *love* old rafters, warming pans and stuff.' He ran a finger along a beam. 'Muck!' he cried. 'Just wait, I'll have this place a little palace. A real little palace, boys!'

And so he did. Robert rubbed and scrubbed and polished and

buffed until paint shone, brass dazzled and the whole ship stank of wax polish like some high class bordello. Then one night we all went ashore for a quick half, leaving the bogey-stove alight as usual. Nobody thought to tell Robert the facts of life relating to bogey-stoves.

We got back aboard quite late. The wave of heat met us when we opened the deckhouse door. It washed out over us as if an oven door had been opened, but it stank of paint rather than a batch of scones or a Sunday joint. We went rattling down the companionway in a body, into the saloon and into a choking layer of heat and smoke. Somebody clicked the lights on.

'Bloody HELL!' we chorused.

The bogey-stove was ruby red-hot like an iron Father Christmas and the asbestos board behind it was cooking the wooden bulkhead. Smoke and a palpitating glow of latent heat arose. Robert had stoked up the firebox but left the damper open. We should have told him. Now, he used his initiative. We should have stopped him.

Straight up on deck he went, seized a deck bucket, filled it and straight down the stovepipe went this spitting, hissing flood. The bogey-stove responded with a great whoomph of dust, steam, smoke and cinders – a Vesuvius in miniature. We might have been entombed, artefacts preserved for the delectation of future archaeologists.

We stood there, powdered like shop buns. Robert ran a finger along a beam, examined it, goggled at it.

'Me rafters!' he groaned in deep shock.

He was at the bus stop first thing next morning.

13

Blind Date
She was a big girl, a very well-made girl

I found out what a blind date meant. It means a date you haven't seen, a surprise. Seeing that my mate 'Spoofer' Murray had set it up I shouldn't have been surprised, neither should I have been surprised to see what he'd lined up for his own date.

The rendezvous was the saloon bar. They came in. First this dainty armful with blonde hair over one eye like the girl in the shampoo ads; the pout, the sizzle that sends shirt-tails shuttling up and down spines like roller blinds; then her companion. 'My blind date,' I divined with stoical resignation.

Biceps, legs like a pool table, heavy black eyebrows, a handbag the size of a shopping trolley. She probably pumped iron. Why not tossed cabers? I thought bitterly.

'My friend Joan,' said Miss Shampoo whose name doesn't much matter. Spoof and I half rose, nodded and subsided with olde tyme gallantry. They drank gin-and-lemons with a thirst like a scavenge pump that left little room for

My boyhood buddy 'Spoofer' Murray. When engaged in subterfuge and villainy his voice rose half an octave.

45

intellectual congress. Buying them drinks was like topping up a boiler, eye-on-gauge, and while it was an investment in carnal cooperation which their mother's wouldn't like, their mothers weren't going to get it.

It was my shout again. I sorted my folding money with mounting concern. Plainly it was time for The Walk. I semaphored Spoof with my eyebrows behind their backs. He nodded.

'It feels stuffy in here, what about a little walk to get a breath of fresh air, girls?' Spoof said in the slightly piping voice he used when up to no good. They knocked back their drinks and got to their feet with an alacrity that boded ill.

Spoofer and Miss Shampoo led the way. The path climbed up into bluebell woods, the haunt of pipit and yaffle or lesser spotted woodpecker – facts which I pointed out to Joan.

'Yeah?' she said.

'In springtime there is a carpet of bluebells as far as the eye can reach!' I said, interestingly.

'Yeah, that right?' Joan said, plodding determinedly.

Ahead of us, the other couple stopped. There was this boggy bit. Spoofer swung his fair companion up in his arms. We heard her laughing cry of protest as he strode forward to firmer ground where he set her down. My heart sank.

We reached the boggy bit and Joan stopped, shifted her grip on that enormous handbag and waited. There was nothing for it.

'I think I'd better er carry you um Joan,' I said, trying to inject a merry note into my voice. Lord Lucan ordering the Light Brigade to charge probably sounded more lighthearted. Joan beamed, assumed a sort of half-crouch like a Sumo wrestler and waited expectantly.

It was like lifting, with the intention of carrying, a washing machine. I couldn't get a grip. I always seemed to get these big women and they *always* expected me to carry them. Muscles cracking, features contorted, I got her airborne.

'Whoops!' she cried delightedly, 'Now then...!'

I took one staggering step forward and my feet sank. In vain I attempted to pull them out of that quagmire. My legs gave out. I sank forward to a kneeling attitude as though in homage and making an offering. I said *that word*!

Joan, deposited on the mud, struggled to her feet. Her handbag fetched me a clout.

'There are *ladies present*!' she said witheringly.

Mortified, I made some attempt at mopping her down, buttocks and thighs. It was not the wisest of moves...

'I think maybe I'd better take you back um Joan!' I said when a gap in her rhetoric allowed. It made her sound like an unsatisfactory purchase, which in a way, considering all those gin-and-lemons, it was.

14

Duty Free
What to do with excess booze? Pay up, drink up or dump it?

Holland is leaking in a manner of speaking,
In spite of the seawalls they've dug;
And small boys hang about,
With one finger stuck out,
Looking for holes to plug.

Back in the fifties the Island Cruising Club of Salcombe mainly attracted nervous beginners, who were also plucky when you think about it and consider the heaving, heeling environment of our massive gaff-rigged cruisers.

When three Proper Yachtsmen in Proper Yachting shoes, caps and oilskins arrived we heaved sighs of relief. It would make a pleasant change from total tyros in sandshoes and belted macs. (One of whom had even brought his own deckchair.)

'What time does the boat dock?' he asked, settling himself comfortably for the voyage.

With three Proper Yachtsmen in the crew, sheets and halliards would be manned by experts and our normally serpentine wake would straighten out. We would have knowlegeable fellow sailors to yarn with on watch and our dinghies would no longer disgrace us in port. There would be boatmanship. No more backwards-sitting, crab-catching muffins ramming everything in sight. Chance would be a fine thing.

As hoped, the threesome proved to be highly competent, they rushed around heave-hoing and coiling ropes with every appearance of informed behaviour. We were sailing the Brixham trawler *Provident*, eighty tons of pitch pine, hemp and tanned canvas, but if she seemed foreign to them after their own tiny boats, they gave no hint. They were racing men who saw the old trawler as an embodiment of obsolete inefficiency.

48

'Have you ever raced skipper?' one asked.

'Only with an egg and a spoon,' I said, laughing uproariously at my own wit. There was a silence.

Theirs was a world of sailing flat out, heel-and-toe athletes with pumping elbows, chins-in bums-out. *Provident*'s comfortable lurching progress was like an old easy chair compared to chrome-and-black-plastic posture seating.

I laid a course for Guernsey or somewhere near, our course being dictated by what she would lie when full and bye.

At once the three of them started sighting up the masts and headsail luffs, thumping the shrouds and swigging on sheets.

'You haven't got a slot skipper,' one accused me disturbingly, 'Look at that luff! And you've no kicking strop to take the twist out of your mainsail!'

In no time at all they had her strapped in tight like a stretcher case and as my old mentor fisherman Les would have said, 'Lookin' but going no-bloody-where!'

It was all a sorry disappointment.

Our cruising itinerary included a stop in St Peter Port, Guernsey to stock up with cheap Duty Free gin and cigarettes, then on along the North Brittany coast, round Ushant and as far as time permitted

Ilton Castle, *ex-RAF launch and one-time dinghy sailing base of the Island Cruising Club, Salcombe. The arrow indicates the toilet flush tank on deck. When the chain was pulled, if you waited the user would come up on deck and refill it with a bucket; then you knew who'd been in there. There wasn't a hell of a lot to do in Salcombe in those days.*

down to North Biscay and home.

Ordinarily, the personal allowance we were able to take back into the UK was a pint of hard stuff and two hundred cigarettes, but with a couple of weeks of cruising ahead, the usual plan was to stock up with enough to see us through without touching our Duty Free rations. We were unlikely to drink ourselves rigid, an evening tot and a nip at lunchtime was hardly debauchery. It meant an extra bottle and another hundred snouts.

Our three bold mariners came back aboard clinking and clanking like a brewer's dray. They had the makings of a smoke cloud like the *Royal Scot* leaving York. You'd have thought we were bound for some Temperance world gushing with orange squashes, inhabited by deep-breathing vegetarians. 'Don't worry,' they said when I reminded them of the modest allowance permitted, 'Don't worry skipper, *we're on holiday*!'

We sailed for Morlaix where our vast bowsprit won us first choice of berths inside, as might a charge with fixed bayonet and a hard eye. The Shipping Forecast whipped the smiles off our faces. An area of Atlantic low pressure was deepening and moving rapidly east.

'Drink up, we're sailing!' I said. We locked out and motor-sailed hard for L'Aber-Wrac'h, the last shelter before rounding Ushant, which is the out-thrust elbow of Europe, aimed at the kidneys of pink northerners heading south for the sun.

We came up with the entrance to the river at dusk. 'Gales in all sea areas!' said the shipping bulletin cheerily. What should I do, hole up in L'Aber-Wrac'h and listen to howling rigging and drumming rain, interminable Scrabble, booze and snout? Have a shot at rounding the land and berth alongside in Brest? The latter sounded more attractive. People could go shopping for the

Quimper ashtrays which were the standard expression of gratitude to neighbours for feeding the cat.

So I laid close-hauled to the west, Doing the Wrong Thing with the practised ease of the cock-up exponent. I had missed my chance. Almost at once a thin drizzle and a strengthening wind made plain the error of my decision. There came a hard squall that made the old trawler stagger and drew from our rigging a deep throbbing moan, as though she was trying to tell me something as indeed she was. I thought to myself, Sleightholme what the hell are you doing?

The night turned ugly. The barometer was pitching and we could no longer lie the course I had set. The waters of Ushant are a wilderness of rocks and riptides which can run at eight knots; in bad weather; *it is not a place for pleasure.* I wiped the rain and spray from my eyes. What now? The entrance to L'Aber-Wrac'h is strewn with reefs, well buoyed if you can see them, but could we be sure in this howling murk? A small error, a misread tidal set could drown the lot of us!

I made a token attempt to find the off-lying buoys but failed. We heard the Ile Vierge lighthouse siren but saw nothing. Once the black-on-grey mass of a great rock appeared and was gone again, then I chickened out. I laid her head offshore and hove-to.

I was sitting hunched over the chart. A man came in looking scared. 'Can't you get us in? We ought to be in somewhere!'

'It's an adventure. You paid for adventures,' I told him.

'Oh,' he said.

We were hove-to on port tack which meant that our head-reaching and the nor'east-going tide would in time set us athwart one of the busiest shipping lanes in the world. An adventure I could well do without.

By now we were snugged down with two reefs in the main and mizzen, small jib at the stem-head and foresail stowed. We lay broad-off and despite the racket of what had become gale force, it was not uncomfortable. With a becket on the wheel and a deckhouse lookout, we lounged below and listened. Joyce had a great pan of stew simmering. Thus must many a winter blow have been passed in the days of sailing trawlers.

The stove was alight, she lay with her shoulder down as we rolled from vertical to thirty degrees, each roll accompanind by a deep shuddering sough of wind through wood and wire. Occasionally there came a boom and a rattle of spray across the deck.

The night passed and merged with what looked like grey

porridge. Nothing was to be seen except the endless ranks of waves marching down on us, a grey desolation, unpleasantly frightening, like most adventures. It blew all day, a moderate gale, nothing to bother our trawler, we could draw sheets and get going, somewhere, whenever we chose. But where? We could run off up-Channel back to the islands. The St Malo corner was as ugly a lee shore as one could find. Nobody fancied it. We would stay hove-to and hope for the weather to change.

It didn't.

Once, in the night, there came a mighty clanking and there appeared, rain-blurred, rows and tiers of lights and wet steel and a boiling of water as the ship rushed upon us, hung above us and clanking and thudding, crossed our bows mere yards away. Her stern light hung upon the night like the grin of the Cheshire cat and as mocking. 'Bugger this,' I said, 'we're a sitting duck!'

So we drew sheets and I laid a course for where Lizard Head ought to be and we headed back across-Channel.

My conscience troubled me a bit. Should I have gone back inshore and tried again to round the land or at least braved the forbidding approaches to L'Aber-Wrac'h? A seaman's gut-reaction told me to stay the hell away from such a coast in bad weather.

Nobody had complained about my decision to head back across-Channel. Life hove-to had been pretty revolting. A huge sea had sent us shooting up and down like a fiddler's elbow – down below everything had been streaming with condensation, both loos reeked of stale vomit and all the other human miasmas; stale food, armpits, diesel oil and bilge water. The ship's company was hacked-off, shaken up like a lucky dip, the milk of human kindness well on the way to becoming full-cream butter.

> *Oh I'm not going down to the sea again;*
> *The way of the whale I've forsook it;*
> *And the only horizon I've laid eyes on,*
> *Is the rim of a galvanized bucket.*

With the passage of the last low, the wind had veered north of west which gave us a close fetch for the Lizard, seventy miles away. I started the mainsheet a bit, half-weathered the clew of the staysail and with a loose becket on the top spoke of the wheel, let her find her own way. She made a gently undulating course like a drunk. Our Proper Yachtsmen, scandalised, remonstrated with me.

'For heaven's sake man, what are you playing at? We need a skilled helmsman in these conditions, let us take over!'

'You're welcome to keep lookout but keep your hands off the helm,' I said. 'Watch and learn.' Which went down a treat.

We stormed along all day, raising the Lizard light loom at dusk and bearing away for Plymouth soon after, which meant that our racing helmsmen could get their hands on the wheel because she wouldn't steer herself so broad-off. Without intending to, I wiped the smiles off their chops.

'It's a pity about all our extra booze and stuff,' I said. 'We'll either have to cough up the Duty, surrender it or ditch it!'

'Or drink it, or drink it!' they chorused, spluttering, indignant and deeply incensed by the injustice of the system. 'Those bastards won't get their hands on it! Come on boys, let's have a party!'

All I could do was persuade them to stay below. We left a wake of cigarettes. They drank around half their excess booze, dumped the rest and then snored indignantly all night.

We went ranting into Plymouth Cattewater with a livid dawn, our decks still streaming, our rigging throbbing and a great boil of wave at our bow. There was a visiting French naval vessel, the watchman had his binoculars on us and as we stormed past he went to the wing of his bridge and swung his arm up in salute – not to us but to the old trawler and sail and tradition. It was a moment to remember.

Another moment to remember came when the Customs' launch came alongside and the officer, with the Power of The Crown at his elbow, dealt with the tricky matter of excess. He listened to my heart-rending tale of storm and tribulation, of our honest intentions, of our sheer abhorrence at the very idea of defrauding HM The Queen of her cut. He thought for a very long time.

'The way I see it,' he said at last, 'is that these things can happen.' He had a way of looking at you under his eyebrows. '*Once!*' He was a master of the pregnant pause... 'If these things happen *twice* however, the Book gets thrown at you. Right?'

And he let us hang on to our excess. Not everybody aboard was delirious with joy.

15

Breaking the Ice
Talking about teeth...

When I was a charter yacht skipper the worst part of a new cruise was the supper on the eve of departure. You've got eight to ten silent novices sitting around a saloon table, listening to the rigging aloft clunking against the masts and the gurgle and splash of water, and they're wondering why the hell they are there and will they be seasick, wrecked or hit an iceberg?

It's like a dentist's waiting room with people reading *Country Life* upside down or gloomily exploring teeth and gums with tongues. It is the skipper's job to distract them from their dark

You pull knob 'A' whereupon away goes lifebuoy, rope, quoit, a yellow smoke canister, dodgers port and starboard, dinghy, cockpit cushions, wife's shorts and two tea towels. And you think you've got troubles!

forebodings and in fact what better topic than teeth? Everybody had a personal anecdote about teeth and dentists. Just get them started. So I would tell them my own horrible tale.

When I was a little boy, I would say, the school nit-nurse would come and while she was at it she'd take a gander at our teeth. It was a high-class school. This old biddy in her white coat told my mother that I only needed two small fillings.

'Oh good,' mother said, as if this was a rare treat of some sort. It didn't fool me because I knew that mother was scared witless of dentists.

Well the appointment came a week later. The school dentist had his workshop in the back bedroom of a back-street house smelling of boiled cabbage, oh very stylish. There was a framed diploma on one wall and a picture of The Teddy Bear's Picnic on another, doubtless hung there to set at rest the minds of the young. 'Oh great!' I thought, 'Picnicking bloody teddy bears, well that *must* be alright then!'

The dentist was tall and skinny and he stood there swaying like a bus conductor. He said, 'Ah, come in young shir!' 'Young *Shir*?' I thought. 'This bloke is half-pissed!' I was a discerning child. Mother hadn't noticed. She stood there smirking the smirk she reserved for posh people like bank managers, priests and doctors who were what she called 'cultivated', implying that they had been reared in an incubator like day-old chicks.

Well he got me into his chair and started staggering around knocking things over and humming a little tune, stoned out of his skull but mother just stood there beaming, her not being in that chair. There I sat, gob open while he poked around dum-de-dum-de-dum.

'Jush a little prish, prick,' he says.

This was probably what the harpoonist said to Moby Dick, 'just a little prick!' Wow, if that goddam syringe had had a hundred fathoms of line on it I'd have taken the lot! I hollered and hooted.

'There now,' he says, sitting down on his treadle contraption and starting to peddle.

Many years later during the war, I was fortunate enough to see a travelling Grand Opera Company perform in Portsmouth. I had never been to the opera and it was plain to see that I had missed a treat, it was also plain to see why they were travelling. Five soldiers, singing, marched round and round a rocking plywood castle, making out that they were an army. Then there was Marguerite, built like a Sumo wrestler, sitting at her spinning wheel hollering and pedalling fit to bust. Crash! It folded up like a trick fire screen and she went base-over-apex. I had not appreciated Grand Opera until then.

My dentist's contraption didn't collapse but it hurt like hell and I'd had enough, I wanted out, the hell with spit-in-the-bowl and teddy bears. I made for the door, which was when mother suddenly wised up to the state he was in.

She ate school inspector's for breakfast. She dismantled him. She took him apart like an educational toy. She threatened to have him skinned and hung out to dry. We left.

Well my story had its usual effect and soon everybody was talking about impacted wisdom teeth, abscesses and drilled nerves. All except this one pale little man in very long shorts who was buttering a cream cracker.

'What about you Jack,' (Charlie or Norman, who cares?) I said, laughing healthily, 'haven't you got a toothy tale?'

The cream cracker broke and he buttered the palm of his hand. 'I *am* a dentist,' he said.

16

The Dark Tavern
There are doors which are best left unopened

This is an uneasy little story. My parents had moved to a small Devon port where they rented rooms in an old waterfront building, which had once been a sailor's tavern. It was closed down by the law because of its evil reputation – that was a couple of centuries ago. It was H Certificate stuff, disappearing travellers whose naked corpses were found rolling seawards on the night ebb, screams, bloodstains – all very dramatic.

My mother regarded it with relish. She was religious but neither po-faced nor happy-clappy about it. She was on familiar terms with saints and angels and free with the holy water, which she dashed around any new abode like Jeyes Fluid.

As a child I had even been taught what to do should I meet up with an 'unclean spirit'. I was to hold up anything handy in the form of a cross and say, firmly, 'In the name of God what wantest thou of me?' The occasion had never arisen, had it done so I would have run like the clappers, I certainly wouldn't have said 'wantest thou'.

My current girlfriend and I paid them a weekend visit and caught the full blast of mother's revived interest in the occult. It was a big, rambling old building now lived in by its owners who rented out the half they didn't need. He was an ex-square-rig sailorman with the missing fingers to prove it, and she was a chintz-scarf sort of woman and a medium – which got mother going right away. 'Having a toe in the door to the spirit world and in view of the "vibrations" that must be emanating from a place with so dark a past, surely she must have had some uneasy experiences?' mother wanted to know.

'No my dear. There are doors which one opens at one's peril!'

She had even put on a seance for mother's benefit but it was spoiled by husband John who came shuffling in with tea and biscuits. She had just contacted her familiar, Chief Sitting Bull.

'Ah! You could have done me great harm!' she roared, coming crashing down off the Astral Plane.

Mother undismayed, had her nose to the trail. In all, there were six of us present that night. Mother was excited due to a mysterious bird which had appeared at a window several nights in succession. It was large, swan-sized but short-necked and despite its fluttering against the glass as if trying to break its way in, it had been completely silent. An omen?

She decided that with six of us we could try an Ouija board. It was of course grossly irresponsible because on occasion, an Ouija board is potentially fatal, like hunting for gas-leaks with a lighted candle.

There was a polished and circular table. She cut out the alphabet in cardboard letters, arranged them in a circle and set a wine glass in the centre. We all sat around, each with a finger on the glass, grinning a bit self-consciously. Candlelight, shadows, the rain needling against the window. None of us took it too seriously at that stage, although we all felt a faint sense of unease. Mother began the business.

'Is there anybody there?'

Nothing happened. Somebody giggled and mother frowned.

'We've got to try to be serious.' Sorry.

'Is there anybody out there?' We waited, fingers on the glass but still nothing happened.

'Give us a sign.'

Did the glass rock? Or were we all wanting something to happen? Mother got specific.

'Are you man?' Nothing.

'Are you woman?' Nothing. So she asked the question which should not have been asked. We were tiring a little, our arms were aching and the night rain needled the window like invisible claws. Mother said, 'Then what are you?'

There was no pause: suddenly the glass was in motion, sweeping to and fro across the table, our fingers, our arms following it, not pushing but following it.

'B-E-A-S-T!!'

We sat there rigid. Mother made the sign of the cross. 'What wantest thou?' We threw ourselves back from the table.

Papa le Mer
An old man of the sea

We left *Hoshi* at anchor off Lézardrieux and caught the bus to Paimpol, once home port to the schooner fleet which fished cod off the Grand Banks of Newfoundland. You could still see old men with claws for hands, frostbitten from hand-lining in their dories on those foggy, freezing banks.

We once passed two of those old boys fishing in a dory. At the sight of *Hoshi*'s schooner rig, they both stood up in their wobbly little boat and saluted her for they were schooner men who had long forgotten the miseries and remembered only the magic.

It was when we were looking for a bus to return that we met the wife of Papa le Mer. 'Can I help you?' said a Welsh voice, a

(Left and next page) Hoshi*'s sails were cotton, pre-war and ripe. Joyce and I never stopped cobbling them.*

From Salcome to Scilly a stitching we come, our fingers are sore and we're stiff in the bum.

lilting voice from the val-lies. She found us a bus and joined us on it for she lived across the river from Lézardrieux.

'We must visit and meet Papa,' she said, 'He is The Old Man of the Sea!' Then she told us how she had come to meet and then marry him. It was a larger-than-life tale.

When the first German troops marched into the village it was with the usual bombast, goose-stepping jackboots, chins up and stoney-faced for the benefit of the watching peasants. One of those watching peasants was the young Papa le Mer, a feisty fisherman and very angry indeed. He stepped forward into the path of the conquerors, folded his arms and scowled. He let the front rank come within reach, then he swung up a real nose-buster, turned and ran like hell. The element of surprise – and a storm trooper with his hooter spouting gore is very surprised indeed – gave Papa a head start.

He lost his pursuers and hid in a cave. Once darkness came he rowed to England. The closest point is eighty sea-miles, nearer one hundred to Plymouth, where he fetched up. He spoke no English

but he was quickly digested into the Free French Navy where he met a young Welsh nurse who spoke the Welsh language and very easily conversed with Breton-speaking Papa, which was not his real name at all at that time. They married.

We paid our social call. Papa proved to be short, squat and long of arm. He had a spherical head and intensely blue eyes beneath his jutting eyebrows.

It was a bungalow in the French style, one room opening into another – this proved disconcerting when you needed the loo, which I very soon did in consequence of the volume of rough wine pressed upon us. Papa was not allowed spirits – his heart – but wine was good for you. His wife translated for him. He told me of his fishing days, how men paid for a chance to serve as lighthouse keepers on the Roches Douvres where crayfish and lobster swarmed in their multitudes. 'It was a dreadful place for mariners, a place of death and I must go nowhere near it, for the rocks drew like a magnet!'

This cheery bit of pilotage information came as no surprise.

The rocks and Barnouic to the south of them lie midway between Guernsey and the north Brittany coast, combing the rushing east-west tidal flow which lies athwart the course from Guernsey to the Trieux River and Lézardrieux. This was our usual route with Island Cruising Club cruises; Guernsey, to stock up on cheap booze then Brittany to the rivers. Therefore I knew the Roches Douvres all too well and feared it in foggy weather.

'Papa says you must never go east of Roches Douvres in fog because then your compass goes crazy!' said wife Mary. There is a magnetic anomaly in that region, where iron on the seabed plays hell with compass magnetism. I believe that nowadays it is shown on the chart, but there was no mention of it then.

Papa had his eyes boring into mine, he shook his head 'Non!' he said 'Non!' and he wagged not just his finger but his hand and arm, 'NON!' he asserted yet again for good measure. I got the point. 'Non!' I said, and meant it at the time.

While Joyce and Mary washed the dishes, Papa took me to see his boat on the shore below. We followed a narrow, steep and winding path to a small cove. Papa talked continually, shouted rather, in Breton, volume being necessary to ensure that a stupid Englishman might understand him. I replied with 'Oui' in various tones and modulations.

The boat turned out to be a typical carvel-built one, some sixteen feet in length and of prodigious weight. She went to sea no more, he explained, with much down-turning of his mouth and spreading of hands, 'Finis, finis!'

'Ah finis!' I mourned, rolling my eyes in a heart-breaking fashion. Papa then put a finger to his lips, saying 'Shhhh!' and casting ominous glances upwards towards the bungalow and, I presumed, Mary. He looked left and then right. He moved aft to a small locker hidden under a sack, which he removed and folded prior to producing a small key and opening the locker. It contained a bottle of Calvados and a glass, which he wiped with his sleeve before passing it to me.

Hard stuff was strictly forbidden on account of his weak heart. He held the bottle by its neck and swigged hard, filled my glass, said 'Chizz' which I took to mean 'Cheers', and was probably the only English he had managed to pick up and swigged hard a second time. It was like being kicked in the gullet. We nodded and smiled a lot, sitting there in the sunshine.

By using sign language, he indicated that the wicked stuff in the Calvados bottle was *local* Calvados; local apples, crushed by stamping with sabot-shod local feet.

We returned a month later and I sent a postcard from St Peter Port, Guernsey to say that we were hoping, weather permitting, to reach Lézardrieux in a couple of days time.

'You needn't have done that,' Mary said, 'Papa always knows when you pass Roches Douvres. He's The Old Man of the Sea!' Perhaps I should have paid more attention to her remark.

Entering the yacht basin, St Peter Port, Guernsey. There is a half-tide sill. A triple hazard of deep keel, faulty arithmetic and obscured tide gauges (which are metric anyway), awaits the stranger, who is alert to the possibility of an abrupt stop and a great jangling of tin mast. An opportunity to practise his British sang froid, which sounds like some sort of wind instrument.

Papa had a special treat for me, a jar of pickled ormers, which are a sort of shellfish peculiar to those waters. They looked like bottled ears, greyish and completely revolting. Neither was his munificence at an end; shyly he produced a bottle of his own home-made Calvados and if it had been produced at a doctor's command, you would have shot the horse.

I thanked him fulsomely and ditched both as soon as I could safely do so since the ormers looked as though they would light up at night, and a mental picture of Breton sabots stomping through the cow-shit en route for pounding apples to pulp did nothing for my taste buds.

It was the Autumn before we were back again and this time it was by a different route: we had visited the island of Jersey by way of change, and consequently approached the Pontreux River from a different direction. To use the clock-face analogy, instead of approaching from twelve o'clock we came in from three o'clock – from the eastern side of the Roches Douvres and the Plateau de Barnouic which Papa had warned about in fog.

It was a quiet and pleasantly warm day, hazy but certainly not foggy and as the day wore on, the towers on both Roches Douvres and Barnouic became visible on the starboard bow. I took bearings, laid the fix on the chart and instructed the watch to tell me when the towers came into transit. Then, being off watch, quite happily I went below to lie down for a spell with a good book. This, as I should have known, is as effective a means of getting to sleep as a rap over the head with a rubber cosh. I had a stress-dream in which a huge mouth was yelling in my ear. What it was saying I couldn't make out but it was urgent and I woke with a jerk, dribbling over my book. I went on deck.

All was peaceful. Lazy conversation, the helmsman lazily fisting the wheel spokes, the old yacht lolloping along nice and easy with an occasional whirring from the patent log on our stern. But there was no sign of either of the towers. There came the deep note of a foghorn. The watch simply hadn't noticed that haze had become mist – fog!

I ranted a bit. The foghorn came again and this time I timed it; sixty seconds to the next blast, Roches Douvres. The direction was wrong though, it was fine on the starboard bow and by now it should have been broad on the beam. How?

'I haven't been more than a couple of degrees off course!' the helmsman said defensively.

'Shut up. Listen!' I said holding my hand up for silence. We listened. 'There!'

Faintly, on the *port* bow, came the mooing of a whistle-buoy. I felt a cold chill of unease. It was intermittent but unmistakably a whistle-buoy. I looked at the chart. There was only one whistle-buoy and it was beyond Barnouic. The inference of the two sound signals could only be that we were heading directly for the reefs, or between them?

Sound in foggy conditions can play tricks. You get 'lanes of silence' when sound leap-frogs – or is lost or amplifies. You cannot rely upon bearings taken of sounds, yet supposing our compass course had been screwed up by deviation, such as a magnetic anomaly? Supposing we had been fifty or more degrees off course?

I took over the helm and turned her until the whistle-buoy was broad on our starboard bow. 'Steer that.'

I got the hand-lead – for we had no echo sounders then – and I took a cast but found no bottom at twenty fathoms. I heard no sound of squalling seagulls or surge of wave to indicate that rocks were close. We sailed on.

Gradually the wheezing of the buoy passed aft to our starboard quarter, grew fainter and was heard no more. The tide was now hurrying us west and the sea's surface puckered and swirled.

'Look. What's that?' somebody cried.

A tower materialised on our port bow and I knew it well for it was La Horaine tower and beyond it, suddenly, the whole panorama of river and rock became visible and we were safe.

Mary greeted us warmly enough but Papa scowled. 'He says you are a naughty lad. He says it is foggy and you came the wrong way!'

That was the last time we saw either of them. It was ten months before we were back. Club members wanted new cruising waters; we headed further west round Ushant. It was late in the summer before we returned to Lézardrieux and climbed the hill to the bungalow.

It was empty, weeds grew in the path. Windows stared with blank eyes. There was just one more place to look. We turned and clambered down the narrow path to the water.

The boat had gone and grass sprouted where the shape of her lay, and that was more final than anything. We never saw or heard from them again.

18

Not a Proper Reporter
How I damn nearly got thrown in the dock

I've yet to meet anybody who regretted becoming a yachting journalist. I was luckier than I deserved.

I was in my mid-thirties, a career catastrophe; my sole qualification, a certificate for swimming forty yards on my back and a similar distance on my front, awarded upon leaving school at age fourteen. I had neither trade nor profession – other than being the unqualified skipper of an under-equipped and parish-rigged holiday yacht. I was like Little Boy Blue, commanded to 'wind up my horn', the sheep being in the meadow and the cows in the corn – an agricultural cock-up to be sorted out by an incompetent in a sailor suit, armed with a tin trumpet.

Then came this opportunity to join the editorial staff of *Yachts and Yachting* and to become a journalist. It was offered partly, I think, on the strength of a few written words but mainly because I had married a girl who had once been editor Bill Smart's surrogate daughter. Joyce had joined the magazine straight from school; I had snatched her off to sea and put her in the family way – she must be properly provided for.

As skipper and cook/mate, with a paying crew of fluffy innocents, we had bashed around the Brittany coast for year after year, literally *stitching* our way along as the ancient pre-war cotton sails split and gaped. A clapped-out engine, no radio, liferaft nor lifejackets and two thirty-year-old rockets on sticks as our sole concession to safety added up to luck being pushed beyond the limit. It was high time to move on and Joyce's condition was the catalyst.

That she got in the club in the first place was a miracle comparable to the Virgin Birth. In order to leave two 'paying' berths vacant and to give us, as young marrieds, somewhere private to have the occasional bloody good row, we elected to sleep in the sail locker where there was not one inch of level space and the headroom was only belly-button high. The two bunks I had built were eighteen inches wide and hard up under the deckhead. I reckon our daughter was conceived midway between the two hundred gallon fresh water tank and the stopped-up storm tri-sail.

It was when she was some three months gone that we were run down by a Royal Mail liner, which is another story (*A Funny Old Life*, Adlard Coles Nautical). It was time.

One morning I received a telegram from Joy's mum, it read: 'Joyce gone into shrubbery to have baby stop'. It was fortunate that I knew The Shrubbery to be a maternity home and not some bizarre form of natural birth.

To begin with, and in a panic, I moved into a near-derelict, condemned two-room cottage where I squatted with the owner's connivance and five quid's worth of junk furniture. We lived frugally but happily; then came the job offer. Mother took over baby Michele

The mighty Creole, *then owned by Greek shipping magnate, Stavros Niarchos. She was loaned to take part in the first Tall Ship's Race, Torbay to Lisbon.*

which meant that Joy could have her old job back on *Yachts and Yachting* until we had recouped our fortunes. She went ahead and I followed two months later.

I was conscious of my salt-bleached wardrobe and particularly my lack of A Proper Suit. For years I had worn sweaters and jeans, I had an off-the-peg yachting jacket that fitted me like a fire-blanket over the back of a chair. On arrival in Southend-on-Sea, where the magazine offices were, I sought out a tailor.

He was a tiny man like one of Snow White's dwarfs who had to stand on a box to measure me; he should have erected scaffolding and worn a hard hat. It was like a sculptor working on a statue. He asked whether I wanted a single or a double breasted cut. 'Think big Sleightholme,' I told myself and ordered the double.

I ended up looking like a Russian Secret Policeman. There should have been a big felt hat and black boots. You could have leaned that suit up against the wall like a suit of armour. When hung up in the wardrobe, it looked like some clandestine lover hiding from a vengeful husband. Joyce said it looked 'funny round the neck'. So does a Galapagos tortoise. Having confronted my reflection in a shop window I wore it only for interviews and funerals thereafter.

While in the mood for self-glorification, I also bought a yachting cap, believing it to be *de riguer* for yachting journalists, not realising at that time just what a tore-ass bunch of scruffs yachting writers usually were. With the wire stiffener still *in situ*, I felt as if I had a cushion on my head. It dragged up my eyebrows in an expression of permanent surprise and caused me to walk with the erect and swaying grace of an Arabian tribeswoman carrying a jug. Within a matter of weeks I had filleted it, stamped on it and rendered it respectable as a cruising cap, but first came what seemed like my social 'coming-out' and the vindication of my extravagance.

I escorted 'Biddy' Smart, the editor's wife, to Burnham-on-Crouch Regatta, wearing the cap in its original glory; I was not really surprised when the *Tatler* society photographer, cornered us leaning over the sea wall. Biddy was a lady of wicked and corrosive wit. We were studying a launch-load of club dignitaries and their ladies. 'Those are *never* her real tits...' Biddy was musing.

The caption in the *Tatler* was to read 'Mrs Biddy Smart discusses racing prospects with Mr Des Sleightholme etc, etc.' At the time, it all seemed to me as if this must be part of a journalist's working day. This was the way of things to come.

I soon found out that the way of things to come was day after day of two-finger pecking at a clacking old Remington. I was given a filing tray of scribbles headed 'Clubs and Classes' which dealt with the round-the-buoys tedium of dinghy racing.

'Names!' Bill said. 'Get their bloody names spelt right. That's what sells the magazine. Parish pump stuff!' Peck, peck, peck. *Blue Poppet* (Les Dork and Sammy Pringle) were first around the windward mark with *Little Auk* (Jeremy Slapper and Tony Phelps) soon to take the lead yawn, yawn, yawn. The glories of Burnham Regatta were lost and forgotten. I learned that being a yachting journalist was largely a matter of routine enlivened with occasional brief flights on wobbly wings of literary freedom. And outside assignments. My first was not long in coming.

'A Tall Ship's Race,' Bill announced, waving a press release. 'Lads vomiting their way to manhood aboard square-riggers. You've got a berth aboard *Creole*. Torbay to Lisbon via Biscay huh, huh, huh!'

He gave me twelve quid to buy a camera. The man in the shop was instantly aware of my ignorance. 'Set it f8 at 100th and keep your thumb off the lens. Can't go wrong,' he said in words of one syllable. He suggested that I went along to a meeting of his camera club to pick up a few wrinkles, so I did. They met in a room above a pub.

Club business over, minutes correct and voted as such, the members got down to criticising each others snaps. For the previous meeting they had hired a live model. Fishnets and feathers. There was much sucking of teeth. It reminded me of a solitary occasion when I had attended an Adult Education evening art class. A live model sat on a dais. It was a largely male class. She dropped her drapes, we gulped and got drawing. The teacher looked at my sylph. 'No, no, no,' he said discouragingly. 'Look, you've got this great mass poised on this huge spread.' The model snorted, draped her great masses and stalked off stage like a postman with a sack of parcels.

Creole was huge: a five-masted schooner owned by a Greek shipping magnate, Stavros Niarchos. She carried a compliment of lads whose souls were to be done good to by an unspecified amount of heaving and ho'ing, at all hours and in all conditions – the nastier the better. It was the formula made familiar during my Outward Bound Sea School days, (*A Funny Old Life*, Adlard Coles Nautical). 'Eat up lads!' we would tell them. 'Food nourishes the body on the way down and the soul on the way up!'

The real work aboard *Creole* was done by the Greek crew – small, dark, fierce fishermen who did everything at the double, elbowing lads aside in order to clap on. I was told that each of them was supporting a family hierarchy of inlaws and outlaws, all hanging on the hind tit and the sailors were frightened of losing their jammy jobs. I never got to lay so much as a finger on a sheet. Up would dash a dark little man, 'Ay, ay, ay!' So I took photos at f8 100th, thumb well clear.

We rounded Ushant to seaward and bore off for Biscay, but not every entrant did so. According to time and position, there is a quite legitimate inside passage which cuts off a corner. One Swedish topsail schooner commanded by a young naval officer took this inside route. A tabloid reporter at once filed a story about the dare-devil young officer risking young lives amongst the wicked rocks and racing tides etc. It was a stupid bit of sensation mongering which could have ruined a young man's career. It also damn near got me slung overboard in Lisbon.

Also in the race, there was the huge Turkish yacht *Ruyam,* and it

Creole's spinnaker had a sixty-foot pole. When the wind piped up in Biscay the foredeck was declared out-of-bounds.

soon became plain that we were in contention with her. Greek and Turk tend to regard one another with about as much love as two cats in the same string bag. The Turk set his enormous spinnaker and so we set ours. It had a pole sixty feet long.

We ran all day and all night, while the wind freshened and freshened until it was all too plain that something would have to give. The huge pole was bending like a fishing rod. The foredeck was put out of bounds. In charge of our lads was the doyen of ocean racing sailors, Captain John Illingworth RN. 'It will have to come in or we'll lose it!' he proclaimed.

Niarchos came on deck in his dressing gown. He looked at the Turkish yacht now in the lead. 'Lose it!' he said.

The wind eased, so we didn't. Worse than that though, *Ruyam* left us like we were set in concrete and the Greeks went around in deep mourning for the remaining duration of the race.

In Lisbon I moved ashore to an hotel and got on with being Ace Reporter Sleightholme on the trail of the scoop to end all scoops. With my notebook and camera, set at f8 100th, I began a tour of the docked fleet of contestants. With an unerring nose for a story, your intrepid news-hound went aboard a large Swedish barque. At the gangway I was greeted by a barrel-chested young officer with white eyelashes who jerked his chin at me inquiringly.

'Press here,' I said with pride, camera ready at f8 100th.

'So!' he said, 'Eenglisch newspaper yar?'

Coyly, I took this small inaccuracy in my stride. Well I was, in a way. He gestured me to follow him aboard and into a deckhouse where he pointed me to a bench and stood facing, arms folded, scowling and blocking the doorway. A lad was despatched on some errand.

'Um fine ship!' I tried, beaming and nodding. He scowled. Then in came the Captain and a conversation took place in rapid Swedish – not that speed made a hell of a difference to me.

'So you write damn lie in newspaper hey?' the Captain said at last. 'You write bliddy robbish about (name of ship) hey? Maybe a leetle swim for you hey?' I got the message. I cracked. I babbled the truth.

'I'm only a yachting writer, *not a proper reporter!*' I confessed a little bit shrilly.

19

A Cunning Strategy
A small matter of deviation

Oh I must go down to the sea again,
A blue-water sailor I am;
And at Southend pier I'll master my fear,
And go down to the sea by tram.

'Would you skipper her?' the owner asked. 'I can't make it and I don't want the lads to be done out of a race.' I agreed at once.

'What a pity it couldn't have been that simple. I was not all I seemed to be. I had a shameful past. I had once overheard my fellow crew discussing me.

'What a pity *he is really a cruising man!*' somebody said. It hinted at a criminal record and time served for Grievous Bodily Cruising, a dark and slothful past.

Oh I'd been clever, masquerading as a racing man, hurling myself around, coiling and uncoiling rope ends, sprawling on windward side decks or tiptoeing around whispering in calms. In my secret heart though there lurked a cruising man, soft and content to sleep in the more comfortable lee berth.

The racing philosophy is that of the January Sales-goer, get in front when the doors open, use your elbows, grab the half price digital camcorder, bang, bang goes your plastic and away. I had six blokes depending on me for a good hard race and a significant result. They would sure as hell get a result.

The yacht was a forty-footer loaded with gadgets like Christmas. The owner had a weakness for bolt-ons and bear it in mind because I didn't and should have. We never won anything, not even a consolation basket of fruit. There would be the great hiatus of the start, a lot of play with stopwatches and cries of 'What have I got, what have I got?' then Bang we're off, 'Oh well.'

Not relishing a mass start I opted for a 'tactical' one. Ordinarily, you

71

get to the ten minute gun with boats under mainsail only sidling around on the fringes. Crew wearing oily trousers holding coffee mugs. Suddenly genoas break out and the whole lot goes mad. Yells, winches ringing, boiling bow waves and eyes popping. The hell with that!

I opted for the 'timed run' start. You do a dummy reach off and back by stopwatch, then with five, four or three minutes to gun you leave the fracas astern, sailing quietly and smoothly out of it all while the stopwatch jerks around towards zero, tacking time and that final triumphant plunge for the line. Or you could just keep going, forget the vulgar brawling and go cruising.

Which is what I should have done because the damned breeze went flat and we were left so far astern that we looked like the muck-cart. My ears glowed red as if giving warning of a sump-oil deficiency. We had a beat down-Solent in company with one of those ancient, banana-shaped boats you used to see, all winch and willpower, pumping away like a fire engine, crewed by zealots and once-in-a-while when conditions were right, over-all winners loathed by all. We had the cans out by then. I got down to some navigation.

Once outside the Needles Lighthouse there wasn't any; it was a straight cross-Channel, reach for Cherbourg and by God's Grace the apparent wind was so far ahead of the beam that spinnakers could not be carried. I liked spinnakers the way a horseman likes haemorrhoids. Flying a spinnaker is like holding a wild cat by two claws and a tail.

'It's funny,' the helmsman said suddenly, 'All that lot ahead have their spinny's set. They're heading more up-Channel than us!'

I detected a whine of criticism. I stuck my head out and so they were, the whole bloody fleet except us and the banana-boat which was plunging bows under and going nowhere in particular. Why? I went through it on the chart again: tides, possible wind shifts; it didn't figure. Why? Could they have borne off just to be able to set spinnakers? I did the sums again, but drew no comfort. Any gain in speed would be lost in going to leeward and having to beat back.

Was I a man of decision, or was I a wimp who copied the pack? Did I think for myself, follow my own judgement or did I tag along limply, lacking the guts to back my own decisions?

'Steer the course I gave you,' I told the muttering helmsman in a strong, firm voice, setting the trap for my own undoing, donning my fool's cap, caparisoning myself with bladder and bells. The rest of the fleet, pointing a good twenty degrees to leeward of us, bowling fast under spinnakers, faded to become pale ghosts in the fading light of evening. I gulped.

Our course diverged, a lonely furrow ploughed into the gathering shades of night. The mass disapproval of my crew hung like a damp blanket. 'Oh well, that's it then!' somebody said in the brittle silence, a valediction to any remote hope of winning anything other than derision.

Just to show dedication to my responsibilities I got out the radio direction finder and waved it around.

'Barfleur, diddy, da, did-da, da-dit,' I chanted, taking a bearing of the helmsman's earhole. The bearing made nonsense. It wasn't as though I'd never used a RDF set. I had a cheapie one on our own boat which Joyce used for listening to Wimbledon. Night closed in black. Once there came a great clanking bundle of lights that blew a raspberry at us and disappeared.

Dawn broke, although it needn't have bothered because there was nothing to be seen. Well *almost* nothing. There was a crowd of gulls sitting on what appeared to be a coffee table but which turned out to be a dead sheep, nicely inflated and with four legs stuck up. My plot, my distance-run, indicated that it was about time we saw something more substantial, like say Europe.

Then, 'Land on the port bow!' somebody cried, right on cue.

'Barfleur without much doubt,' I said, trying to keep the triumph out of my voice, tapping the chart. 'The tide is setting to the west'rd. It should set us nicely athwart the Cherbourg easterly entrance. It would never surprise me if we weren't in a nice position.' I added on a small note of pride. I should have kept it shut.

'Tall lighthouse,' the lookout continued. 'Looks to be flashing every five seconds.'

I bent over the chart, pencil tapping. I felt a sort of black busby of doom descend upon my head; my ears registered low battery and a fault in the circuit. The lighthouse could only be Cap de la Hague, some eighteen miles *to the west of Cherbourg*! It was like a boxer taking a swing and laying out the referee.

Worse still the tide was carrying us rapidly across the Alderney Race towards Alderney itself!

The crew showed neither sympathy nor surprise at the situation, only a sort of piggish pleasure at my undoing, an 'Aw well what did we expect?' attitude. Then came my deliverance, the exquisite revelation that got me off the hook and back on top; the cruising man vindicated.

'We might just as well make for bloody Alderney!' somebody said. 'At least we can try out Denis's new echo sounder.'

I pounced. 'And *where is this new echo sounder?*' I gritted.

Oh I must go down to the sea again,
I've taken mummy's advice;
We may get a shower in the next half hour,
Then I think it might turn out nice.

It was mounted on the bulkhead to hinge out into the cockpit. It was exactly behind and a thickness of plywood away from the steering compass, exerting a deviational force that made a twenty degree error as certain as bread falling jam-side down.

It was like being crowned queen of the fairies.

20

Circulation Figures
We tended to be coy, like ladies discussing hip-sizes

Nowadays circulation figures are not easily fudged, not as they once were. Magazine circulation figures are the broad-sword wielded by Advertising Departments in hacking out a share of the advertisement market. When I first joined *Yachting Monthly* we were selling, actually selling for hard cash a little over 20,000 copies which I quickly learned, tongue firmly in cheek, to enhance by another 10,000.

Then there was the Post Office receipt scam whereby, at regular intervals, you sent out free copies to everybody from the highest down to the ship's cat. Thus the crofter in his remote and howling wilderness, birthing lambs in the light of a tallow dip, received his yachting magazine, delivered by a cursing postman through snowdrifts.

Rival magazines disputed one another's figures and enhanced their own. Dodgy readership surveys added percentage figures like icing and little silver balls. 'Sixty-eighty percent of readers questioned own detached houses,' they'd claim, basing it on a total sample of twenty, knobbled outside Harrods. Your circulation figures were not to be discussed in polite society, like how much you earned and haemorrhoids at supper.

A leading Swedish engine manufacturer, big-time advertiser, was promoting a new model so come ye all, bow down and adore it – if you're hoping for a lick at the lolly. An invitation went out to yachting magazine editors and their equals, six of us in all, very high powered stuff. You didn't send your junior with the office Cannon slung around his neck eager to get at the free booze. The Advertising Director sunk his fangs into my trousers and I went.

Heathrow Executive lounge and aquavit, executive jet, aquavit and coffee over the North Sea. Hotel with freebies, Company sweatshirt and Company Parker pen, aquavit. A stretch limo took us to the factory where young execs with white hair – a career necessity signifying total dedication to work – tongue-lashed us on the merits of the new engine and handed out the glossies. 'Tonight we haf fon!' said a young exec.

It was low season in Stockholm, by then dark, chilly and belting down with rain. We were all tired and needed our beds; what we got was Tivoli Gardens Amusement Park and 'fon'. Apart from one small family with newspapers on their heads, it was empty. Our guide bought a wodge of tickets to cover every attraction on offer. We fired at things, threw things, munched wet candyfloss, whirled in dank discomfort on Dodgem and Big Dipper and ended up in the Tunnel of Love and Oh what fon!

There was no restraining us that night, I tell you. Madness was in the air. Six men, middle-aged to ancient, in pairs, rumbling through the fusty darkness. I shared a car with old Frank and his Vic inhaler. Out popped a ghost woooooo, the signal, on more usual occasions for squeals and cuddles. 'Bugger this!' Frank said, sniffing.

All good things must end though, and it was time for dinner. We dined lavishly in a black cellar where the menus were two feet square and totally unintelligible. Waitresses had skirts like economy lampshades and bulged. They bent over and we didn't know where to look, which is not strictly accurate. We ate fish and longed for bed. Horlicks would have been nice.

'Now we find a nightclub and some birds and haf fon!' declared our gaoler. Another black cellar, this time with music, a thumping beat at a decibel score to rival a trip-hammer foundry. Drinks were five quid a kick and the birds were clad minimally in black fishnets. Frank had one on his knee. He still had his muffler on, and he was peering around her bulges like an engine driver looking for signals ahead.

The following morning we were given a tour of the factory. We wore our Company sweatshirts like worshippers at some solemn ritual, machine-shop, test-bed, coffee, aquavit and sales-spiel. Then lunch, for which we shed sweatshirts and donned our reefers. The venue was on an island a high-speed boat trip away among rocks.

We learned how aquavit *should* be drunk which was not via the pursed lip and a maidenly sipping as Frank did it, but with a click of the heels, a jerk of the head and a cry of 'Skoll!' Straight down. It made for a limited conversation. 'Skoll, Skoll!' we chorused, clicking and jerking. Laughter boomed. It always booms when men are getting stoned out of their skolls.

There must have been a meal although I cannot recall one. Raw

Adrian Morgan modelling a finger. We were doing an article about Not Shouting, aimed at husbands with wives on foredecks. In fact they just go below and then he knows what he can do with his boathook.

herrings and brown bread maybe, with chilly glasses of still chillier hock and more aquavit. And toasts.

We toasted our respective countries, each other, the Company and magazines, the chef and the kitchen cat. 'Skoll!' we croaked, swaying and clutching the table. A wine glass went over, God it was funny, *fonny*! We beamed, scarlet-faced, ties awry. Our hosts smiled thinly. I was just about to toast Stockholm – all of it, when our top host, with whiter hair than anybody else, rapped the table.

'Now,' he said, smiling at me the way Count Dracula might have smiled while eyeing a promising jugular vein, 'now to business. *What is your circulation, sir?*'

There was the sort of silence you might expect when mentioning nooses in the house of the hanged man. The room was suddenly stricken with silence.

'Ah', I said, 'Yes ah...well!'

21

The Upside-down Course
Being back by Monday morning

'You have been hoist by your own petard,' somebody told me, who had literary inclinations. It sounded like some sort of car jack until it was explained that it meant being blown up by your own bomb – a fair description of what happened.

We had this sleep walker aboard who had come sailing to recuperate from having been dropped on his head. We were on passage from Chichester to Biscay, quiet and easy sailing, doing it in one leg. He was sharing the fo'c's'le with me. I was skipper. The second night out he went ambling aft to the wheel where my wife Joyce was presiding. He leaned over confidentially and said, 'There is something foul in the fo'c's'le!' Nobody guessed he was sleepwalking. It sounded reasonable. He just ambled back again.

It happened again the next night, only this time his secret was out because he was snoring as well. What was to be done about it? You have to be careful not to wake a sleep walker in case he or she does something foolish, although blundering around snoring is hardly the sign of the intellectual giant. Being the skipper, though, I must deal with the matter wisely and conclusively.

I rigged a booby trap – a petard. We were sleeping with the forehatch open on account of the quiet weather so I rigged a taut line across it which, I reasoned, would wake him if he tried leaving. I went off watch and turned in. Somebody stuck his great daft turnip head down the hatch and whispered loudly,

'Skipper, would you like to take a look at this!'

Never mind what 'this' was, it could have been a sea serpent or a mucky photo. Up I shot. It was the wing-mirror/garage door effect, 'DOYNG!' and my bloody ear was left humming like a tuning fork. There is no justice; I meant well.

'We meant well!' Thus it is with we yachting magazine writers, holding forth interminably on how this or that should be done, all with much wagging of fingers, gratuitous advice which we ourselves often ignore. We are the physicians who pour our own medicine down the pan.

One of my pet themes was about the folly of taking risks in order to get back to work on time. I wrote a ditty:

It's not rock and reef that causes the grief,
It's ignoring the weather warning;
We pay it no heed and crack on at speed,
To get back by Monday morning.

Which was more or less what I did in our own plump little cruiser that horrible summer, years after that petard-hoisting episode when I had meant well.

We had hammered our way down-Channel like Easter Penitents on suffering kneecaps, anchoring tenuously for the night behind anything that promised a bit of a lee, flushed out by a shifting wind again and again with two inches of pyjama stuck out from our oily trousers wicking it up. We had made it as far as Salcombe where we lay on our anchor playing Scrabble and listening to shipping forecasts, a dizzy itinerary conducted to the drumming of rain and my lamentations, when Joyce made her classic pronouncement.

'Oh for God's sake,' she howled, 'you're on holiday, *enjoy it!*'

We started back in plenty of time, or so it seemed. We even chanced our arms with a quick dash across to Alderney, where the wind went nor'easterly which is straight into the harbour, and set us rearing and plunging. We went ashore and viewed the fortifications, which is to say we staggered around them bent double and spitting sand.

Slowly we clawed back up-Channel. The wind shot back into the sou'west as we reached the Isle of Wight and Monday morning loomed. We had to get back to the river Orwell in Suffolk.

'We'll do it in one,' I said.

You don't make statements of that ilk when you are sailing. The Fates home in on you, 'Oh will you,' they say, 'Is that right, do it in one, will you?' You just shouldn't make that sort of statement.

Ordinarily we'd work watch-and-watch – me navigating and Joyce rustling up grub as needed – three-on, three-off. Not this time. The wind fell light, and our speed fell from five to three knots which is about as fast as Nanny with her pushchair. From Wight to Dover is 100 miles.

At Dover Straits there is a tidal node – the tidal streams from North Sea and Channel meet and divide. If you can time it right you can carry the east-going stream to Dover, then nip aboard the north-turning stream and be carried on around the corner 'down-north', as they say. The truth is more like a marital Christmas shopping expedition when you aim to meet up at the coach station. 'I've been standing around like a fool for the last hour,' she says, 'Where the hell have you been!'

Despite our slow progress and the fact that it should have been a gentle coastal passage, we seemed to attract rancour from all angles, like a passenger on a crowded coach with two suitcases and a backpack. I got no rest at all, thus sowing the seeds of a cock-up. Again and again I would be sinking into a health-restoring coma when Joyce would have to call me up.

To use yet another metaphor it was like the *Twelve Days of Christmas*, six trawlers trawling, four crabbers crabbing, five coasters coasting, plus Lords a'leaping and drummers drumming. Every son-of-a-bitch making straight for us, including a clanking

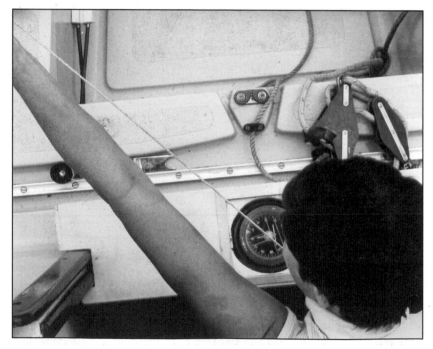

Joyce modelling string. She said, 'Why is it you can only take views of backs of heads and bums; are you freaky or something?'

rust-mountain with Amazonian Registration and a helmsman with (I do not doubt) a bone through his nose.

I was ragged by the time we'd passed Dover and I aimed to go into Ramsgate to catch up on some sleep. If you can't find a berth in the outer harbour you have to lock into the marina though, which could mean time wasted waiting for the gates to open. It was dusk as we passed through the Gull Channel. Ramsgate came up and suddenly I felt bright and alert, keen to press on, all tiredness forgotten. This is a phenomenon that I knew of old, a dog that licks your hand then bites it. Beware the second-wind where fatigue is concerned, but I didn't.

So we went on and rounded the North Foreland with the wind at sou'west and a fine sandy bottom and we ranted and we roared as the old song goes. Tongue Sand then Princes Channel, across the mouth of the Thames Estuary with its one hundred lights and more, all winking away dementedly. We had a nice port fetch now, speed up to five knots again.

'Get your head down, I'm fine!' I told Joyce.

Somewhere between East and North Tongue buoys the dog bit. Suddenly weariness washed over me. My head slumped until my teeth met the tiller and I jerked awake again. I lit my pipe. I decided to put the Autohelm on, which was the worst thing I could have done but I had the North Pan buoy flashing five seconds red fine on my starboard bow, I could doze.

With the Autohelm on I could go below and lay a safe course to cross the tail of Kentish Flats. There was shipping to watch for but that would keep me awake. The course I plotted was 275° magnetic. Between the chart table and the grid steering compass, wearily climbing the companionway steps, yawningly peering down at the compass and setting the ring, my 275° somehow became 257°, easy as that.

We passed the North Tongue buoy. From there to the Pan Sand is a couple of miles, say half an hour. Half an hour slumped against the cockpit coaming, rolling to the motion, senses hovering between sleep and wakefulness and the soft swish of water, the sigh of a night wind hushing me deeper into oblivion.

There came a rush of water and a heavy lurch, a slap of breaking and another rush, a tremendous crashing impact as the keel struck. Joyce came up, crying out something.

I had the bows off, mainsheet free'd. BANG and a kick from the tiller as the rudder hit. Then suddenly, thank God, she was off and the snarling of water fell astern.

I said to myself 'Oh you bloody, bloody fool!'

There would come times of equal weariness but never again did I try to navigate. I leave that to the nerds of this world. I'll stick to pilotage.

A Drop of Fresh Water
You can wash from head to foot in a pint of fresh water

I have never done so, or even attempted it, although the drumming of knees and elbows coming from the loo and the vile language to be heard on occasions leads me to believe that other people may attempt this frugal feat. One pint of water is applied presumably with fingertips or a reeking flannel is hardly likely to produce a scrubbed and healthy body; socially acceptable and ready for tennis.

The marina hose has meant that tanks are kept full – save for some Continental marinas where local owners have their own connectors. Visiting Brits leave empty-tanked or must grovel for the loan of one. In any case it is traditional for sea-farers to be short of fresh water.

First thing in the morning people use the loo in hot-seat succession, abluting with cries of 'Aghhhh!' At least the men do. The women *glide* in and out with long spells in between, and nobody ever sees them enter or leave. When somebody is in the loo for a wash, others *listen*.

Father, guardian of fresh water supplies, counts the fresh water pump strokes. 'Eleven, twelve, *thirteen*!' he counts in tones tremulous with indignation. Somebody is due for an ear-wigging. 'Do they think we're on the mains or WHAT?'

Our 'fresh' water tanks, after a brisk turn to windward, either yield a foul sludge which is all right when boiled (we comfort ourselves), or it reeks of styrene, but we thank God for filtration and sip tea of indescribable foulness.

Past generations of yachtsmen with dribbling canvas water-carriers, knocked on the back doors of remote cottages having walked a mile in both directions. They knew the meaning of economy and they cooked in saltwater without fear of nuclear power station fall-out making their ears light up. They also had their lather-free saltwater soap that nobody ever used after the first attempt.

I knew an owner who was a fresh water Scrooge. He lived aboard and washed seldom, his clothes never. Accordingly, he built up a great quantity of foul sweaters, revolting shirts and underwear that you'd expect to handle with blacksmith's tongs – that's if you ever got close enough.

He was cruising abroad and moored to a jetty of sorts where he found, to his delight that there was a tap and a length of hose. He went ape. He topped up his tanks and every container from jerry can to saucepan, then he scrubbed decks and topsides, filled the cockpit and washed his sails, followed by every garment he wasn't actually wearing at the time, and with numerous changes of water. Finally, he stripped off and, also in the cockpit, starting at his feet, he washed his whole person.

All that day his boat lay there with rigging festooned with drying sails and garments – shirts swooped and pirouetted, long johns pedalled, pyjamas cavorted. Finally, when all was dry, he got under way before anybody should arrive to relieve him of any money. Not that they would, seeing that the water was rated unfit for drinking and for having a notorious effect on the bowels.

23

A Matter of Trust
Not a tale to be proud of

At the end of a race, when the party is over, when club ties have been amputated in drunken fervour and all the speeches are over, the boats have to be returned to base. Which is when a lot of crews, owners included, find that they are urgently needed back in their offices. So skeleton crews sail the boats home while the rest catch the ferry.

'Seeing that you are senior in years and sea time, will you skipper her?' the owner asked me. There were three of us, the other two were regular crew, and I was an occasional pier-head jumper.

It had been a Portsmouth to Dinard race, which meant St Malo. We set off home late on Sunday afternoon. There was no wind and it looked like a smooth and boring engine job. The race had been anything but boring. We'd had a spinnaker run down through the Channel Islands and out around the Plateau des Minquiers with its million rocks. Fog had closed down as we left Jersey. As a cruising yachtsman my gut reaction had been to dowse the spinnaker and either lay a wide course around the 'Minkies' or get the hell out altogether and go somewhere safer.

We'd had to find the outer buoys. If we'd gone *inside* them, leaving them to starboard we would have been doomed. The navigator had worn a worried frown like a screw-top jar. Our spinnaker floated, ghost-like overhead with skeins of fog swirling about it. The lookout gripped the bow pulpit and stared ahead into sweet damn-all. Condensation dripped; the water hissed and gurgled under our stem. To me it was sheer lunacy; it was also racing.

We heard – or thought we heard the SW Minky buoy, a throaty aspiration described on the chart as 'whis'. Tensed up, hands raised demanding silence, we strained our ears but never heard it again. The navigator ran his distance and ordered a change of course with the air of a gambler staking the family fortune on the turn of a dice. But it had been OK, we had finished the race without disaster or disgrace.

Oh I must go down to the sea again,
Though it isn't a restful sport;
And the bunk I must lay on,
Isn't easy to stay on,
Being triangular, narrow and short.

Now we were doing lone two-hour watches. The engine droned on and on. The fog had gone and you could see the wide-ranging lights of buoys and beacons, and it was smooth and easy going. I sang as I steered. Singing to an engine, above the clattering and whizzing of innumerable mechanical bits means that your voice becomes a mellifluous baritone, heard at no other time. 'Some enchanted evening...' I howled. I was almost sorry to go off watch.

I slept with engine-induced profundity and when it stopped suddenly, I was instantly wide awake. The sounds told me that the man on watch was topping up the fuel tank from the reserve jerry cans carried in the cockpit lockers. Then came the starter motor, repeatedly, on and on and on.

I arrived on deck to find both my watch-mates up there and a hell of a row in progress. The other off-watch crewman was raving mad.

'The bloody fool has only topped us up from the *fresh water jerry can!*' he bellowed.

The fresh water can was painted white to distinguish it from the green fuel cans; he hadn't known this – jerry cans meant fuel. It was no good bawling him out, the damage was done. We had neither thetools nor the skill to strip down bits of engine and drain the tank.

'We'd best get her sailing,' I said.

It was about 2am on Monday morning, and we had around ninety miles to go for the Needles. Under the big ghoster and hard on the port tack we were making about half a knot, a rate of progress comparable to queueing for the last bus. It looked like eight days of sailing.

I felt an uneasy stirring; I had an important boot-licking job scheduled for Wednesday. When a magazine editorial offends an important advertiser, the editor eats crow and sends a journalist armed with a camera 'to show interest'.

'Pic and caption,' warns the editor, 'You're not writing *War and Peace*.' He holds up narrowed fingertips as an indication of caption length, I shuddered at the thought of the editor's wrath.

The tidal atlas for the waters of the Channel Islands and adjacent coast of France showed a horde of little arrows hurrying north between the islands. They reached a point in the Alderney Race, and milled around uncertainly, like rail commuters told that the seventeen-fifty at platform ten is now arriving at platform four. They stampede south again. Which is why getting clear of the Channel Isles in a calm, and in an engineless vessel, was ripe with potential cock-ups.

During the following twelve hours, we brought *Sark* abeam to the west and stood still throughout the south-going stream. Then the breeze freshened from gnat's breath to force two, and by Monday evening we were entering the mouth of the Alderney Race, where the tide went foul and we were stuck again.

When in the Alderney Race the water seethes and gurgles, it puckers and swirls, spinning you 180 degrees and back, and either you shoot through holding a useless tiller, or you are stuck – or you go backwards. In bad weather you'd better be somewhere else.

We sheered as close as we dare to the island, and foot-by-foot got as far as Blanchard Shoal but no further. There was one rock that became hatefully familiar. It was like the man in the banged-out red Cortina in a two-lane traffic crawl.

Tuesday morning found us shot out with force by the north-going tide, tiring of us like visiting relatives and wanting to get shot of us.

We were all three anxious about our delayed return. We had no radio in those days and certainly no mobiles; we were as cut off from the world as ancient mariners. There was nothing to be done but to concentrate on sailing the boat with all the skill we could muster. Light-air racing was no comparison. We watched the lazy cat's-paws that darkened the shimmering sea, willing them to head in our direction, while the sails overhead shished and shushed to the slow roll.

We inched across the shipping lanes where the majestic leviathans, triumphs of design and masters of the oceans, passed in succession. They looked like a block of flats followed by a row of lock-up garages. One had the temerity to give us a blast of his horn.

By dusk, the Isle of Wight lay thirty miles nor'east of us, a recumbent humped form like a drunk on a park bench. All night we ghosted, helmsmen sprawled along the lee cockpit coaming, fingertip steering, keeping her going, speaking in whispers, watching the Needles light double-occulting through the pulpit rails. It grew from a loom to a hard speck of light, losing the battle with the dawn.

We reached the Needles Channel predictably as the tide turned foul, then it was like trying to battle up the wrong escalator with no time to study the Pretty Polly advertisements. At 10 am on Wednesday we entered the Solent where we kedged in total calm.

I hoped that editor Bill, once a racing man, would have got the charts out. He had been a heavy-weight boxer, MTB skipper, cavalryman and ocean racing pioneer. It was his pleasure to follow my racing progress in comfort in the office. He'd spread charts over his desk. The worse the weather the keener his enjoyment, 'Force eight on the nose huh, huh, huh!'

I hoped he would hunch what had happened and grit his teeth and phone the griping bastard I was supposed to be placating.

Day-long we inched up the Solent to the mouth of the Hamble where a yard launch put us on our trot. It was late afternoon on Wednesday, a three-day passage. Then I committed my fatal blunder. I wanted to phone my office and Joyce, to put her mind at rest, and phone the owner. We had a hasty clean up, grabbed our kit and got a lift ashore. One of the other crew, a regular and a good shipmate, put his hand on my arm.

'Get going, Des,' he said. 'Leave it to me, I'll tell Peter (the owner) and I'll come down tomorrow, clean up properly and get the yard to work on the engine!'

And I believed him. In fact he did *nothing*!

If only the owner had raved and cursed me but he just said, very quietly, 'I trusted you!' Three words which have haunted me all my life, for the blame was mine: I was the skipper.

A Lyme Bay Cock-up
We had this gut feeling, we were heading into trouble

Offshore racing yachts are demanding on their owners who can't always take it; ours had been niggly right from the start. Maybe it was the prospect of a rough race? Some people have only to take a look over the sea wall and they bring up.

It was a Lyme Bay Buoy race with a Southsea start and a rushed one. We'd all done a day's work, dashed down to Portsmouth, rushed afloat, let go forr'd, let go aft and straight to sea. Ideally you should start a race with a rested body and a serene mind. An hour's vigil kneeling before a candle wouldn't do any harm.

Southsea starts were right on the beach where it is very steep-to. You slice to and fro, heading onshore, then round you go with a shrilling of winches and off again. Bathers see a bow wave with ten tons of yacht behind it boiling in at them, and they quit the water in a blur of pounding kneecaps.

Our skipper was unusually beastly and his voice rose to a hateful squeak, which we ignored. Then we were off, well back in the crowd, covered by just about everybody else. It was rough going and having once buried our bows they stayed buried.

The course was round a buoy off Cherbourg, back across-Channel to round the Lyme Bay buoy (long-since removed). Then outside the Wight and back to the start.

I found myself off watch and so I turned in at once, which is what you do when it is rough. It gets you out of the way, filed for future use. It is like being hustled into bed by a brick-jawed hospital ward nurse when you are feeling fine.

The yacht being flat on her ear, Sod's Law allocated me to a weather settee, to which I clung precariously. My bum made a pregnant bulge in the lee cloth. This meant that those forced to squeeze past, being cold, wet and on watch (and therefore vindictive), gave it a good old prod in passing.

In such conditions, actual sleep is as elusive as the pea in the thimble trick. It is a patchwork of nightmares woven around the sounds of water, wind, thuds and shouts. To the busy subconscious it is a phantasmagoria, a precursor of doom. 'Wha', what, what!' croaks the sleeper struggling upright and braining himself on the bunk above. It was dark when I awoke and I felt dreadful.

The owner was also in a state of great agitation having identified a Class III budget boat ahead and to windward, which is a situation akin to owning a Merc and finding the last parking slot occupied by a Reliant Robin. He wouldn't turn in until we'd put her astern and rounded the buoy.

We'd had a seventy-mile close fetch on starboard – a car-wash of wind and salt. We plunged around with a great yammer of winches, sails blattering and slamming and three or four other yachts vying to be the inside boat. Yells and curses. Ashore, the lights of Cherbourg glittered like red embers. Waterfront cafés beckoned, aperitifs and cashew nuts, 'Would Monsieur care to order?' 'Square that bloody jib off!' and away we went again into the black of night sustained by a mug of stewed steak and beans, a yawn and a shiver.

She went away like a young colt turned loose in a paddock, kicked up her heels and galloped. She roared off, boom clipping wave crests, rudder drumming, rigging taut and singing. She left a wake of easy curves, the way it should be on a reach, letting the rudder follow the ship rather than fighting her.

The owner wouldn't turn in. The sleigh-ride went on all night, with a succession of helmsmen beaming, as though personally responsible for such magnificent sailing, and him sitting hunched over the chart table. He had the bearing compass cupped in both hands like a crystal ball – Gypsy Rose Lee with stubble – wittering about our curvacious course. 'Oh, oh, oh...throwing the race away!' and so forth.

Nowadays there is no Lyme Bay buoy and so no race, and perhaps it is unmourned because it took some finding.

You had your Beme Loop to get a radio beacon cross. The navigator turned it this way and that, listening to squeaks, getting a bearing that made no sense unless the helmsman was dead on the heading at that instant. So the helmsman sat up there gripping the helm, white-knuckled with concentration, chanting 'On-on-on' or 'Off-off-off'. Then he'd go right off. 'Oh shit off, no, on-on-on!' It was like playing a fruit machine. An orange and two lemons! Getting a good enough cross to pinpoint a small object like a buoy in the middle of nothing was asking for miracles in windy murk or fog. It was like the Belgian National sport of cowpat betting.

No other nation does it. You have a field and you put a cow in it, then you lay bets as to where it will drop its first pat. Contestants spend hours in conjecture and wager large sums. The Lyme Bay buoy was similarly elusive but with a difference, if you couldn't find it, you could 'round its geographical position'. Reliable crew members then signed the logbook and the race was resumed with an easy conscience.

The sleigh-ride lasted all night and then the wind dropped around dawn and we slowed to a wallowing crawl. The owner, who had slept for a couple of hours, arose and resumed his non-stop harangue of the crew. We exchanged glances, rolled our eyes and duly ignored him.

We ran our distance, did the thing with the Beme Loop, applied tide, drift and set, leeway and a bit extra for luck, said sod-it and did a box search – more a packet than a box – a penny-packet of two tacks a gybe, rounded-where-the-cow-pat-ought-to-be, signed the log and then got on with the business.

The drizzle gradually gave way to rain and then wind again. With darkness we came abeam of Portland Bill. There were three or four other yachts in sight, standing out in stark silhouette as the lighthouse beam stroked them; pale as moths in candlelight. The owner stared and sorrowed, they could only be boats with a dangerously lower rating than ours.

George and I went on at midnight, by which time St Albans Head was abeam five miles. Astern, the four winks of Portland Bill peered over our shoulders like somebody having a cheap read of your paper. The wind and sea were dead astern and it was a mucky night with the yacht tumbling around like a drunk. It was a hell of a job to steer – wave-surging, griping, arm-cracking work.

It was too wild to carry a spinnaker, which would have been wrapped twice around everything, so we had the genoa boomed out to port, mainsail to starboard on a foreguy. Which meant that with every wave-surge she griped hard to port. Up popped the owner's head from the companionway.

'You're not on the course I gave you, steer the course I ordered, you're luffing inshore!'

'We bloody-can't!' George told him in no uncertain tone. 'Why can't we gybe on to starboard now and get a bit of searoom?'

The owner went ape.

'And throw the race away, is that what you want? Chuck it in, go skitting halfway across the ****ing Channel?' He vanished and slammed the hatch shut.

'And a merry Christmas one and all!' George said.

Dead ahead about twenty miles, the Isle of Wight barred our course. The Dorset coast lay to port. It was like walking along a pavement or sidewalk with a wall on your left and a heap of rubble blocking the way ahead. You would have to step out into the road – the English Channel – to get round it eventually so why not head out a bit now?

There came another wild wave-glissade and my arms ached with the strain as I heaved on the tiller. We made yet another lurch off course and another few yards inshore. Ahead and on our starboard bow, the loom of St Catherine's light grew clearer between the rain squalls. It should have been on our port bow. The ghosts of a thousand wrecked mariners breathed in my ear. It was *on our starboard bow*!

St Catherine's Lighthouse is low down at the foot of the cliffs, although in ancient times a beacon fire was tended by a lone monk high up on the downland, where the miserable westerly blast of wind and rain obscured it most of the time. The job was probably a punishment for earthly misdemeanours. A succession of friars, not visibly affected by guilt, soaking wet and in vile humour would have struggled to ignite and keep alight a soggy pile of furze.

It was a warning which was needed urgently. The coastline below it has been a ship's graveyard throughout history with the dreaded Atherfield Ledge conspicuous as a ship-killer. St Catherine's light has a red sector guarding it.

Meanwhile we continued to drive surging and swerving, edging off course, eating the miles, swerving and surging towards that terrible place. I stuck my head down the hatch and begged the owner to think again. Gybe us, let us head out of the trap into which we were hurrying. He said, 'I'm trying to win a race, I'm trying to win a race!' as though providing a carbon copy of his idiotic statement.

'He won't budge George!' I reported. I took over the helm and he had a go, head down hatch, a yelling match.

'The stupid sod won't budge!' George said.

We were simply not used to defying our skippers. We might argue tactics, but you didn't show defiance, that wasn't how it worked; the skipper and owner of the boat was in total charge and what he ordered you to do *was done*.

We were by then maybe five miles – not being able to take a look at the chart, it was a guess – from the island shore and with the sweeping beam of the light *on our wrong bow*. Minutes passed.

I had the helm and something was wrong. 'George look! The light...'

The beam of the light had blurred then suddenly turned red!

'Oh Christ!' A prayer.

We didn't pause. He raced forward to cast off the boom foreguy, I had the tiller against my buttock, arms free to haul on the mainsheet...shoving the helm across... 'Gybe-O!' Over she went, above the arcing bow the red light circled, the noise of threshing ropes and a blast of spray; then I was wrestling with the tiller, and George was getting the boom off the genoa.

She was now back in harness and the red light was changing back to white. Where was the owner though?

He was in his bunk, sobbing.

I can only think that he was a sick man, or he had suffered some trauma. He stayed in his bunk. I never sailed with him again.

The Ancient Mud
As if something was pulling me down...

Oh I must go down to the sea again,
To get away from the bricks and mortar;
And I'll stroll by the shore,
Where the great breakers roar,
And get both bloody boots full with water.

My mate Keith, being an aeronautical engineer, was not much concerned by occcult matters; and anything you couldn't measure with a micrometer, or for which a suitable box spanner couldn't be found, did not greatly worry him. There was one strange exception, and perhaps it proves the rule. He told me the following yarn as we lay at anchor in Sharfleet Creek.

Soon after the outbreak of World War II, Keith was an Aircraftsman in the Royal Air Force and stationed in Belgium. He was on sentry duty one cold, raw night and patrolling the bank of a canal. After a while, he saw another sentry who appeared to be guarding the same section. Their paths crossed which seemed odd.

Keith waited until the other sentry approached. Like himself he was wearing a service greatcoat with the collar turned up so that his features were not visible.

'Wotcher chum,' Keith greeted, 'bloody miserable old night!' There was no answer. Surly sod, thought Keith. He tried again.

'What mob are you with then?' This time Keith got a response.

'The Connaught Rangers' (*I believe this was the name*), he mumbled and turning, walked away. That was all but it stuck in Keith's mind. But then came the chaos of Dunkirk to expunge it and some years passed before the incident returned to haunt him.

Keith fell seriously ill. Major surgery was involved and it was touch-and-go. There came a night of crisis. Keith told me what happened almost apologetically, as though involvement with the supernatural was somehow shameful.

'I remember having this dream. I was back on sentry duty on that canal bank and there was this same squaddy only this time it was him who did the talking.

He said, 'Come on back to our billet mate, we've got a brew going, drop o' the hard stuff in it. Come on mate, come on...'

'I knew that I *must not go!*' Keith said. 'I knew that if I went with him I would go out of this world!'

When he was fully recovered he wrote to the War Office to find out about the Connaught Rangers. The answer he received shocked him. A unit of the Connaught Rangers had been stationed on that canal bank in the First World War. They had been wiped out to the last man.

What happened on the mud left me wondering whether Keith was quite so materialistic as he would have liked to be.

There is an area of the Medway marshes that has an uneasy reputation, it was once a place of dark deeds. It is a place of bones. Nowadays medical students learn their bones with the aid of plastic skeletons which are hygienic and easy-to-clean, 'Get new, double-power Ozo for a sparkling coccyx.'

Keith, headless, modelling a heaving line. He heaved the wrong bit and it fell at his feet, which is how you get heaving lines wrapped around props. It is better to hand heaving lines to people in a proper manner.

Some years ago, however, a group of students were in the Crooked Billet in Leigh-on-Sea bemoaning the cost of skeletons for study. There was this raggity old wild-fowler supping nearby.

'Skillingtons?' he piped up. 'If you young ladies an' ginnlum wants a skillington I'll soon git you one. Fiver, there yer are, can't say no fairer!'

His source of supply it seems was somewhere on the Stangate saltings, for Stangate Creek had once been the place where the infamous prison hulks had lain. Gaol fever and a variety of other killers had kept the death toll high. The corpses were most probably buried where the digging was easy.

The quarantine anchorage was also nearby. Ships of all nationalities, potentially carrying every sort of pestilence, were forced to lie here until proven healthy – or otherwise. The dead were disposed of by night and suitably weighted.

Stangate and Sharfleet Creeks were our favourite destinations at winter weekends. Some people went to Ostend for the Casino, we went to Stangate for grislier prizes.

At some stage in the past the saltings had been drained, 'poldered' by the Dutch and used for grazing sheep. Then the dykes had been breached and the marshes had been flooded again. Where was the lad with the ready finger to plug the hole? The lad whose resourcefulness, whose soggy example had been held up to me in my own boyhood as some sort of role model.

'Hans, you'll be late for school if you don't take your finger out!'

Our great delight was to anchor in winter solitude, wait until the tide was out and then plod the muddy shoreline, eyes down, searching for whatever we might find. We never touched bones. The majority were probably sheep's bones but we were not expert enough to tell one from another. We filled our bucket with strange and knobbly bits, heavily concreted with deposit. Keith might hold up a find. 'This could be a musket flintlock,' he would conjecture, knowing full-well it was more likely to be a Victorian privy latch. There was a strange profusion of clay pipe fragments, Dutch gin bottles and brass fly-buttons, suggestive of over-indulgence followed, with the minimum of delay, by a rush for the lee rail.

This particular day in late December, was about as cheery as a pauper's funeral: all it lacked was the Little Match Girl striking one to try to keep warm and maybe *The Sale of Old Dobbin* as a double bill. There was a slanting grey drizzle, zilch visibility and an early dusk in the offing. It was bloody chilly.

'You can go first,' Keith said with generosity, 'I'll carry the bucket.' We pulled the dinghy up and squelched forth on our archaeological quest. It was a big spring tide that day and the low water run was lower than we had ever seen it, which meant unexplored territory. The gin bottles, baccy pipes and fly buttons began clattering into the bucket. Then came this patch...

Over an area of maybe ten square yards the mud was jet black and littered with fragments of black pottery. Excited, we half filled the bucket. It appeared to be shards of jugs and jars and hinted at a domestic shin-dig of long ago. Crockery flew.

'Where the hell have you been? Look at the goddam time!'

We trudged on, scanning the mud for another hundred yards and then we both became aware that the tide was flooding again and that it was almost too dusk to be able to see what we were doing. We started back.

I was leading. I came to the crockery spot, plodded across it and kept going. Then I heard a curse from Keith just behind me. I looked round. I had crossed that black mud alright, but not Keith. Despite being smaller and lighter than I, he had gone in up to his knees. He fell forward and both his hands and arms had gone in. His language was almost lyrical.

I roared with laughter. There he knelt like a fly on a fly-paper. I said so and made appropriate buzzing noises. Then suddenly I wasn't laughing. Keith's face wore a strangely *doomed* expression. 'Help me mate!' he said. I moved to reach out and I began to sink. You could hear a whisper of moving water from the tide edge; the grey dusk came around us like smoke. 'I can't move!' Keith said.

And I said something stupid, 'Hang on, I'll get the dinghy oars.'

Getting to the dinghy and back was like one of those nightmares when you run on the spot, pursued by some dreadful thing. A spring tide moves fast. It was covering the mud while you watched. 'For Christ's sake get me out!' Keith said, pretending to laugh but with death in his eyes.

With the oars to help, shoved under his arms, we got him out and even salvaged the bucket. We got back on board and he stripped off in the cockpit; I carried spare gear aboard. He got into his sleeping bag and I bunged him full of Bovril. Then he said an odd thing. He said, after thought, 'It was like something was pulling me down, *pulling my feet down!*'

A week or so later I showed the bits of broken pottery to a man in the museum. He asked where I had found them and I told him.

'Probably fourth century Romano-British stuff,' he said. 'Grave-goods and food containers for the journey into the hereafter. You've found yourself a burial site!'

And I remembered Keith's words, *'pulling my feet down!'*

26

A Run Ashore
A night on the town comes home to roost

More women go racing offshore nowadays. The old male con that got women off the helm and into the galley 'where they were happier!' is exploded once and for all and the stern male world of wind and sail is diminished by modern reefing gear and methods. The laddish humour which was centred upon bowel and genitalia in general has had to go. Except in the case of the all-male racing crew.

Which is what this crew was and on a Hook Race of long ago, ending up as they do in a Rotterdam yacht marina. There is an almost ritualistic routine to be followed. On go club ties and reefers, off ashore go crews *en masse* to dine with the owner, who, as like as not, will pick up the tab – which is his way of saying 'thank you lads' for drinking the boat dry of canned ale, cocking up that spinnaker hoist off the West Hinder and losing a winch handle.

All-male crews have been known to forget their age and make bloody nuisances of themselves, throwing bread rolls, eating the flowers and drinking the water in the vases. Decent burgers leave in disgust and sober compatriots talk decently in decent accents and try to melt into the wallpaper.

Our crew behaved impeccably, napkins well tucked in, flies zipped and ties out of the gravy. A boring meal ground to a boring conclusion. 'L'addition, s'il vous plait', 'Thank you very much skipper', 'Don't mention it I'm sure!' Whereupon father and a couple more went back to the boat and crashed out while the rest of us went on the town.

This means you trail from one Micky Mouse Bar and Cabaret to the next, all identical, pitch black and pounding, red back-lighting and drinks that cost a 'phew' and a 'bloody hell'! The resident tarts push their boobs across the table as if marketing Jaffas, and invite you to buy them special drinks which are green or red and about as alcoholic as Horlicks.

It was in one of these joints that we lost our navigator. One moment he was dancing, locked tight to one of these old gallopers, swaying, then he was gone. We shrugged.

We reached the 2 am lidded-eye, totter to the loo, deeply philosophical stage, 'meaning of life – shus, shereoushly ole man', spent up, pished-off and ready for bed. Of the navigator there was still no sign, so we wove our way back aboard and zonked out cold.

By late morning the first signs of life were returning to the moored racing fleet. Hatches slid back and dishevelled figures in string vests, clutching mugs, were rising like bestubbled Aphrodites to blink and blear around. You could almost hear the throbbing of heads like jungle drums. I was aware that the navigator was back and I had vague recollections of song, followed by a lot of noise trying to be noiseless, much self-shushing and then a reverberating descent of the companionway ladder and a groan.

We were sitting in the cockpit, squinting at the searing daylight, clutching our mugs. The navigator was still below and making a curious droning sound. The owner, who had had a healthy night's sleep, was as fresh as a daisy and standing up.

Portholes in loos need curtains to use,'
when berthing in crowded conditions;
Or others nearby with lascivious eye,
May regard them as small televisions.

'Oh dearie me look at this!' he said suddenly.

It wasn't easy because it meant turning our heads and focussing but we did so and were richly rewarded.

Along the marina catwalk came these terrible old toms; a pair of them, painted up like fairground horses, skirts no longer than dog-collars, high heels, speckledy tights and low-cut blouses like frilly cornucopias and about to unload a job-lot of melons.

'Bloody hell!' somebody said.

They were reading the names of the yachts. They bent over, dangerously, to read ours then to our dismay one of them addressed us. We slid down inside our collars and stared at distant chimneys. She had a voice like tearing tin.

'Pardon meesters,' she said, 'we are look for the owner, meester Gayter, ee is 'ere please?'

Well, he wouldn't be, would he? We didn't know any Meester Gayters. We shook our heads with flapping wattles, then groaned in agony.

The other old boot spoke up. 'Meester Navvy Gayter?'

Our owner's face lit up suddenly, with a smirk of dawning comprehension. 'Bear with me ladies, I'll just see if he is at liberty.' He went below. There were groans and much harsh whispering. The words 'no' and 'oh God' were heard repeatedly, followed by language so vile, albeit *sotto voce*, that we blanched beneath our pallor.

We watched them go. From nearby yachts, heads rose from forehatches, crowded portholes, jammed companionways. Down the catwalk they went, Meester Navvy Gayter our sweating, blushing navigator with one little charmer on each arm, two globular bums rotating like bags of marbles.

We gave them a standing ovation. It brought tears to our eyes, a manly roar of encouragement and support.

He seemed likely to need both.

A Little Old Gaffer
She was dilapidated enough to be within our price range

Oh call me early mummy dear,
For the air is soft and balmy;
And I'll varnish the rail midst rain and gale,
An earthquake and perhaps a tsunami.

When you have been without a boat of your own for a year or two you begin to get broody. You start hanging around boatyards like some sort of voyeur, taking guilty peeps through portholes, trying to get a glimpse of somebody's layout. You would never have put a gimballed cooker *there*! On port tack it will be stuck out like a wheelbarrow in a dark alley.

You look for an affordable boat, which means a fairly dilapidated one for sale at a price within limits set by a Finance Committee of two, in bed, on a Sunday morning. Marine Mortgages signed for at boat show coffee tables are all in the future. We don't know about 'making our money work for us', only about working for our money.

We found the boat in a classified advertisement: four hundred quid o.n.o, 4 tons Thames Measurement, gaff rig, 2-3 berths, sttng hdrm, generous inventory, lying Wivenhoe.

Thames Measurement tonnage is a figure arrived at by a potty Victorian formula associated with racing handicaps, and four tons means nearer half that, but it sounds good. Two to three berths meant a pair of settees and a triangular shelf shared by the anchor chain, and bucket toilet and sttng hdrm (sitting headroom) meant a permanent Band-Aid tiara and semi-concussion. A 'generous inventory' would include a paraffin riding light, mildewed cushions and an asbestos mat for making toast. The ad said that she needed 'some work', which meant she was in a hell of a state and consequently ideal.

Wivenhoe, a few miles away, was remote if you didn't have a car.

It was reached from Leigh-on-Sea by a succession of bus and train connections interspersed by long and aching waits, spent reading timetables and advertisements for Bracing Skegness which sounded pretty bloody chilly.

The boat, *Cygnet*, was shored up against a wall, looking as though she'd been there since the Boer War, but beyond her peeling paint her twenty-two foot hull was instantly desirable and though a bit plumpish, a real boat. There was one worry, it was a sizeable one, but once in love no blemish can shake the besotted.

She lay with her port side against the wall and it was mossy with moisture, while her starboard side was exposed to the northeast winds, blowing direct from Bear Island, cold and dry – a withering and pitiless blast.

Her carvel plank seams had opened up like letter boxes. From down below you got a striated view of the harbour and a howling draught. We were undismayed, 'she would take up', which is what all wooden boat buffs say when faced with what nowadays would be regarded as terminal trouble.

A local yacht surveyor wrote the usual report which said in effect that she had opened up something rotten, there was a loose hinge on the galley drawer and don't blame him if he's missed something. We bought her.

I took a week's holiday. I would restore her enough for a passage home to Leigh, where I had a borrowed drying mooring that was awaiting her ladyship. With a car boot to hold all I needed, it would have been simple, but I would have to lug it by hand: the tools, paint, handy bits of wood, vice, clump hammer, rope, scrapers, brushes, and a host of items which could not possibly be needed, but which I knew would be the very things I needed most of all. 'You're not taking THAT!' Joyce said.

I had two bulging holdalls and a bulging backpack. With my arms fully stretched, knees bent, my arse was practically skimming the ground. Joyce helped me to reach the station. 'I'll be down next Saturday,' she said.

Two kids watched my staggering progress, both my hands were occupied, 'Oy mister,' one said, 'psst your fly's undone!'

'Oh thanks, son,' I said, putting my bags down, furtively groping.

There was nothing wrong with my fly. 'Little sods!' I howled, getting black looks from bystanders. It was not a good start.

The railtrack to Wivenhoe is now a footpath and a nature trail, I believe; then it was a branch line with a genial crimson-faced station master-cum-porter who lent me a barrow which meant that I got my load to the waterfront in easy time.

I booked a room at a pub. There were three old men supping ale, the typical East Coast Ancient Britons you can still find; squat, round boiled faces, deeply suspicious of strangers, yet determined to find out what you are up to. So I told them, and they knew the boat. One of the old swine began huffing and shaking, making a sort of phlegmy cackling sound so that I guessed a joke to be coming. It came.

'Don't bend over next 'er topsides, squire,' he said, huffing away, 'If you bends over next 'er topsides she'll likely bite yer bleedin' arse orft!' Two humorists in one day was hard to stomach. So was the pie and chips but the ale was OK.

There followed a frantic week. I burned off the hull and antifouled the bottom, rigged her, got the incredible engine running – the gear lever worked backwards – and I gave the gaping topside seams the old soap treatment. You leave a bar of soap in a sealed tin with a bit of wet sponge for a week which renders it cheesy soft. The aim is to knife it into cracks and seams so that it squeezes out as the wood swells. The baby Moses bobbing down the Nile in his leaky basket, blowing soapy bubbles of protest, may well have pioneered the method.

Joyce arrived, the yard crane lowered us in, I cranked up the incredible engine, a reincarnation of historic significance, I engaged forward gear by hauling the gear-lever aft with a mighty grinding and clashing of gears – for it was what they called 'straight-through' – and we headed down-river banging and farting clouds of blue smoke.

From Wivenhoe to Leigh-on-Sea is about thirty-five miles in total, but your course ducks and dodges down the river Colne, around sandbanks and buoys, through spitway and channel in a never-ending zig-zag between deep and shallow. Which is what sailing the East Coast is all about. The wind was a moderate to fresh easterly, which meant that it was hazy and knife-edged, though weakly sunny in the East Coast manner.

Then the engine cut out. A bang, a cough and it went dead. We just ignored it. In our experience this was what engines did. There is a special quality about the silence that follows cutting an engine and in a newly acquired boat even more so, for you hear the rudder and the lap and smack, creak and rustle all speaking together, telling you new things. We heeled a little. We brought Brightlingsea abeam to port, then the coast rolled aside as though opening a door, there was the bar buoy then we were out on the broad spread of the Wallet.

'We're leaking!' Joyce said, below stowing things.

We were also heeling to starboard, deeply immersing our bad side. Soap was squeezing out in long extrusions, peeled out by the rushing water and leaving gaps. Joyce took the helm so that I could go below. A dozen leaks burbled away. It was the Fountains of Versailles; there should have been cherubs and goddam dolphins. George Frederick Handel could have written the music. There was a steady flood down the topsides, behind the settees and into the bilge.

'What's it look like?' Joyce wanted to know.

'Niagara Falls,' I said.

The bilge pump could just cope, but only just. We could either go back sensibly, or carry on hopefully. Another five miles to the Whitaker Buoy and we could bear away and come upright.

I never gave the engine so much as a thought. For fifty minutes we pumped until the pump choked. I couldn't get the base of the barrel to unscrew. I got the paraffin cooker going and toasted it. Down in the bilge, a deepening black lake grew deeper and noisier, sloshing and sploshing. 'Oh bugger!' I thought. I wrapped a tea-towel around the now-sizzling pump barrel.

'I hope you're not using my towels!' Joyce said, astute and unforgiving, for she knew me.

'Oh no!' I said piously, wrenching two-handed. It yielded. There was a matchstick athwart the clack-valve.

We bumped in the Swin Spitway despite our modest three feet of draught, then we were squaring away up the Swin, topsides lifted and dripping. I set the ancient mottled spinnaker, boomed it on the boathook. Our bow wave rose prattling up the stem and our wake joined in with thudding pintle and creak of tiller.

We stood beaming and happy as our fat little cutter, stubby bowsprit leading, went galloping home.

We were half an hour too late to reach our mooring on the tide. We stuck fifty yards short.

28

The Proper Smock
Flat-seamed and eight-to-the-inch I sewed it

J ust as I got my inventive streak from father, I inherited handicrafts
from mother. 'He's good with his hands,' she used to tell friends,
who would back off warily.

She bought a small hand-loom with the intention of founding a
cottage industry and making us rich. It proved a laborious business.
She wove wavy table mats, book ends and a skirt made of woven
strips joined up. It had a curiously puckered appearance and went
up at the back in a disturbing manner.

My particular craft was called 'sailorising' and included such
decorative productions as an eight-part sennit, ocean-plait, thump
mat and grafting. Not least was the Turk's Head which is a sort of cod-
line bubo or lump that can adorn anything from a bottle neck to a
Bishop's crozier. I tail-spliced, wormed, parcelled and served
anything that stood still but my great love was canvas-work,
'sticking'.

A wooden, gaff-rigged boat lends itself. The mast wears an Eton
collar or 'scoot' where it passes through the deck; bottle-screws wear
canvas knickers and there are dodgers, screens, awnings, wind
scoops and covers everywhere. On a windy night the rapping,
flapping, flogging and cracking of canvas sounds like rounding Cape
Horn. My sheath knife had a canvas sheath which rendered it lethal
whenever I sat down, the deck bucket I made spouted like a water
cart and dribbled down your leg. When I came ashore to a job in an
office I made ditty bags, tote bags and a window blind that would
crash down like Traitor's gate without warning.

'I could make you a golf bag,' I told Joyce generously.

'No,' she said heavily.

I was the only London commuter with a ring-hitched umbrella
handle and a cod-line becket on my briefcase. You'd see looks of
naked envy from fellow commuters. Little did they realise the skills
involved in sailorising. Take sticking canvas.

Flat-seaming a sail is the most difficult and you need skill, stoicism and a high pain threshold. You sit on a low bench, the sail across the knees and tethered against your tugging by a sail-hook. You must wear a heavy apron, impenetrable by the needle or you will sew trousers to sail, which will ruin its set and cause you to walk with a heavy tread.

To sew a flat seam you grasp the needle close to its point, settle the eye in the 'iron' of your leather 'palm' and with a powerful thrust of the wrist, fingers extended, you drive the needle point downwards and upwards. One of three things may happen. The needle may slide smoothly through the canvas; the eye of the needle may miss the 'iron', pierce the leather palm and drive smoothly into your *real* palm; or the needle may wobble, and if you are not wearing a heavy apron it will drive smoothly and deeply into your thigh. At this stage you scream, stagger erect and shoot your leg out. A class of beginners working flat out may look like a Cossack choir. Add a novice wire-splicer and you've got your solo boy soprano.

There was this length of heavy sailcloth knocking around in the office that nobody seemed to want. I needed a good strong wind and waterproof sailing smock; I was racing most weekends, which were wet and windy. Such a smock would also enhance my image as a hard sailing man, eyes narrowed to slits, briar clenched between sturdy brown teeth so I nicked it.

First of all I made a newspaper pattern.

'It's going to look funny round the neck!' said Joyce prophetically. Sadly I ignored her and it did. After hours of sticking, offering up, more sticking and more offering up, it was finished and

I put it on. The neckline was reminiscent of a Galapagos tortoise, it was tight at the elbow which straightened my arms out as though I was about to take flight, and like mother's disturbing skirt it went up at the back.

'What do you think?' I asked Joyce unwisely.

Next came waterproofing. The easy way was to buy some stuff called 'Gnu' which is excellent, but I inclined to the traditional. There was this old recipe requiring cutch which I didn't have. You try a modern yacht chandler for cutch or oak-bark or bullock's blood, all ingredients once used for tanning sails and you'll get one hand clapped on your collar and the other gripping the seat of your pants. I settled for a recipe that required paraffin, boiled linseed oil, red and yellow ochre and a drying-time of one week.

Mark that. One week! I stuck a broom handle through the arms and hung it on the clothesline where it swooped and cavorted night and day like some fiendish apparition from hell. Revellers homeward bound from the pub at 2 am recoiled in dread.

'Mother 'o' God, I'll never touch another drop, so I won't!' they swore. Joyce said 'Get that bloody thing off my line before I cut it down!' It could have done with another week at least. It was a mottled browny-red colour.

The first time I tried it was on an Ostend race and the rest of the lads were plainly envious. Ben, the Flower-pot man, said he wanted one. The rain began after dusk, an ideal test for my new smock. The others put their oilies on but I wore oily trousers and my new smock. I pulled the hood up and heard the rain drumming on it and not one drop penetrated, such was the quality of my workmanship and the efficacy of the waterproofing.

My watch went off at 4 am and it was daylight when I awoke, but that wasn't what woke me, it was the hollering from on deck. Somebody stuck his head down the hatch.

'Sleightholme you bugger, come and look at this lot!' he yelled, sounding very nasty.

I went up. The rain had stopped. Wherever you looked, cockpit cushions, dodgers, the watch-keepers and their clothes, hands and faces, everything was covered in browny-red ochre.

29

Unrated Cruisers
The third class citizens of the racing world

In a club's racing hierarchy the dinghy-boys were regarded as the elite, and the small and unrated cruisers, with their plywood number boards flapping in the breeze, as the oafs in the brown boots. The stigma is the description 'unrated', which implies an absence of marriage lines and whispered consultations about sharing the spare bedroom.

Cruisers were not to be taken seriously; we were the clowns who came bounding into the ring turning cartwheels. Ho, ho, ho. There was the Hon Rating Officer who decided our fates less on mathematical formula than upon such esoteric matters as whether a boat had horsehair or Dunlopillow mattresses.

Most of our cruiser races were port-to-port passages events, about as challenging as a procession of Easter Penitents with candles and black lace headscarves (the women). The aim of getting there first was to get the berth nearest to the ablutions. They started with a derisive hoot from an aerosol horn, to save the cost of a cartridge and you could get as many as six starters, which meant on average one protest, one general recall and a family row. Races finished on a similarly dispiriting note.

> *Oh I must go down to the sea again,*
> *Next Sunday from twelve 'till one;*
> *Then I'll miss the drinks party,*
> *Being cheerful and hearty,*
> *And get back after they've gone.*

Most were family crews of croaking adolescents but there were young-marrieds in identical and badly-knitted bobble hats which sagged down when wet, blindfolding the wearers as though in preparation for being shot at dawn; and there was at least one keen and navy-blue woman, frighteningly fierce and raptor-like in a baseball cap, as if about to dismember rival crews to feed her young.

Joyce and I didn't race much, due to my lamentable lack of competitive spirit. We'd round the weather mark and come off the wind. I would get out baccy pouch and pipe.

'You can put that thing away, *we're racing*!' she would rasp. 'Where's your competitive spirit?' as if this was some kind of high-octane nourishment that I lacked.

Not owning a stopwatch, we timed our starts with an old tin alarm clock. One day it went off as we crossed the line. There were these race officers all shaking their wrist-watches and clapping them to their ears.

There was a general feeling among wives that it was better to let the men race and curse one another, despite having to clean up the pigsty afterwards. The real snag being that men then started getting

My mate Keith modelling a homemade hand lead and looking thoroughly disagreeable. Melt the lead in a cocoa tin and pour it into a wooden mould that leaks and piddles molten metal down your shin like some hound from hell. I told him, 'Smile for pities sake!' He said, 'Huh, so I've got to sell my body now then have I!'

ideas about *buying things*. A spinnaker, a new genoa and self-tailing winches and bang goes your fitted kitchen.

There was one man who bought a new boat. It was very fast, being kidney bean shaped and of extreme fin-and-skeg rudder configuration. He ignored the guiding maxim for boats on drying moorings which is that the base of the ballast keel should be narrow or rounded; his was broad and flat. The boat became tide-girt. This meant that as the tide left her, she laid back on her chain, which held her upright and delicately balanced. He got up for a call of nature, saw the situation and dared not move. He stood on the top step gazing fixedly to his front as if on ceremonial sentry-duty. A bait-digger leaned on his fork, looking up in friendly fashion, 'Mornin' squire,' he said.

'Piff off!' the owner hissed.

The Skippers Only race was an annual club event which Joyce said I ought to go in for. 'It would do you good,' she added illogically, since it was more likely to do me great harm. I had an eerie sense of impending cock-up.

Wives and crews settled to watch from the club, Roman citizens eager for blood. We knew we were likely to make total prats of ourselves and so the start was cautious as though the vicinity of the line was an infected area to be approached only in disinfected boots. I performed my celebrated reach-off-reach-back manoeuvre, thus avoiding any risk of contagion. There wasn't another son-of-a-bitch nearer than sixty yards.

'I'll give 'em something to think about!' I laughed going off on port tack while everybody else was on starboard. Incredibly, the other boats, far ahead and pointing for the windward mark sailed straight into a flat patch, leaving me to go for it as if on wheels.

Round I went, up-spinnaker, down-hope, having hooked it over a crosstree, a shroud to cover my ambitions. The fleet streamed by as though I was taking the salute. There should have been a fast reach followed by a run for the line, but I was fully occupied with poking at a bundle of spinnaker with the boathook, and by the time I had free'd it and scooped it out of the water, I was amazed to see that my smart-arse rivals had been caught aback by a windshift.

It was a miracle. Doubtless watchers would ascribe it to my consummate skill in reading the weather.

'By George!' they'd say, shading their eyes, 'that man's a genius!' I fetched the next buoy on a fast reach, bore off and ran for the line with the pack in pathetic pursuit, sadder and wiser for having tangled with Sleightholme. Laughing grimly, I swept over the finishing line, blowing a kiss to Joyce and the other watchers.

I was so early that the race officers weren't even ready with their gun! Round I came, making for my mooring. The cheers and waving mounted to a crescendo, round I came and made the perfect pick-up. I had the sails down and stowed before the first of my rivals had even reached the line.

She went straight over it. The rest of them went straight over it and then they all came hard on the wind *for the second lap*!

30

A Winter's Tail
Where are your fearnaught trousers and your Union suits?

Many claim that some of our best sailing is to be had in the winter, implying that the rest of it must be pretty bloody. The pleasure of winter sailing is absolute hooey.

'Mmmm, fill your lungs with that air!' Winter yachtsmen tell one another, doing so and then staggering around in paroxysms of coughing. Far from being the ruddy-cheeked pictures of health they imagine, they have pinched, grey faces enlivened only by the blue lips and crimson wattles of ornamental pheasants. They are equalled only by the hermit in his hair-shirt, giving himself a regular damn good hiding.

You get whole families going afloat for their weekly penance. 'The family that shudders together *stays* together,' I remember a touching moment when sailing with a family at West Mersea, where the wind comes straight from Bear Island and meets nothing on the way.

There was this dear little five-year-old girl with dancing curls and rosy cheeks. They'd put her down below; out of the wind, which had all the qualities of a can opener. I stood in the hatchway, surreptitiously trying to get a bit of warm air up my kilt. She was staring up at me with a fixed and unblinking eye. I thought to myself, 'You'll remember this moment all your life, little miss, the howl of the wind and the heave of the boat and the kind and comforting presence of a strong male figure to protect and watch over you. Then she spoke. Pointing a steady finger she said;

'That man' – and her small finger never wavered – 'That man has *purple ears*!'

Much of the problem with winter sailing is that we don't wear the right gear any more. Where are your fearnaught trousers, your Union suit with its platoons of buttons and flap-seat and where are your long-tailed shirts?

You can pay two hundred quid for a pair of triple-sewn, Mega-trousers of 'breathable' ventile fabric, but who wants his trousers puffing and gasping at every exertion? It is all down to the Americans who have sheathed our legs in denim and cut off the tails of our shirts. Worse than that they gave us 'sports' shirts. You get a palm tree on your sternum and it is so short that your clock-and-ornaments are displayed with the prominence of a Finefare Special Offer. Buy one get one free.

Back in the sixties I wrote with passion on the subject.

What, we ask ourselves daringly, has happened to those real old-fashioned working shirts with the fine flowing tail of an arab stallion and the broad vertical stripe that made a man look like the spare bedroom wallpaper?

A Canadian reader was so moved by this that he sent me one. It was ankle-length, flannel and striped. I modelled it standing on the top table at the Erith Yacht Club Men's Supper Night and it made a big impression. The members sang as they laid me to rest.

I resolved to test that shirt in a marine environment. Oakley Creek in the Walton Backwaters was one of my firm favourites. It was only navigable around high water but there remained holes in which you could anchor and remain afloat throughout low water, cut off from the outside world as we know it. It was like locking yourself in the outdoor toilet when the Jehovah's Witnesses come knocking.

I anchored short in my favourite hole where the yacht lay like a toy duck in a basin as the tide drained out of the creek. A mud cliff towered. Crabs peered from their holes with a twitching of metaphoric lace curtains.

Something plopped. I ate my boil-in-the-bag, turned off the heater and climbed into the shirt.

Earlier experiment had shown that due to its narrow dimensions, walking was only possible if one took the tiny tripping steps of a geisha girl, although I lacked the chalky complexion and fan to complete the illusion – which my cap and pipe would have tended to destroy in any event. I had remedied the walking problem by rigging a tricing line from the front of the hem which could be looped over my head, thereby raising it to waist-height and facilitating leg movement.

Wisely, I opted to turn in, although this was not easy in a sleeping

When the North Sea ferry goes up-river to Ipswich her displacement causes the water level to rise and sink sharply... If you are aboard a boat in the marina and on the can it can be alarming.

In the marina you might not have seen her,
You may be using the john;
Your predicament rankles,
As trousers round ankles,
You rush up on deck but she's gone.

bag because the nightshirt tended to rise above my waist like a breeches-buoy. Another poor soul saved.

I had this absurd dream. A ship's siren was bellowing. I awoke and lay there smiling at this impossible concept. The smile dried on my face like shaving-soap. A ship's siren *was* bellowing!

I shucked off my sleeping bag like some monstrous insect quitting its chrysalis.

The catalytic cabin heater stood – not unreasonably – in the middle of the cabin floor, and with one easy swing of my body I enveloped it with my nightshirt, took one faltering stride and crashed to my knees.

'Oh God!' I swore – implored. The siren bellowed again. I made it to the companionway ladder, scrabbled up it into the miserable light of dawn. Steel bows towered.

'Coming!' I cried, clattering up into full view. The coaster, for such it was, began backing off with understandable dispatch.

I thumbed the engine into life, thankful that this was not the old *Cygnet*, kicked the cabin heater off, heaved away on my tricing line in order to facilitate leg movement and went forward at a shambling trot to haul in the anchor.

It was all part of the great camaraderie of the sea. A man in a peaked cap came to the wing of his bridge and gave a warm 'hurrah' as his vessel passed mine.

'Good morning,' I called, standing there, fully triced.

31

Roses on my Sternum
Fashion is a tough mistress

My campaign for longer shirt-tails got nowhere. There was some support from farmers whose market-day fustian ramparts and pork-pie headwear needed a sturdy foundation of flannel; fishermen also, with a raw salt blast whipping up their transoms, looked with favour on a long tail.

Elsewhere, fashion dominated the scene and gave rise to that horrid phenomenon know as 'builder's bum.' A sports shirt and jeans struggle in vain for a finger-hold, like some mountaineer with only one piton, leaving an expanse of pinky-grey flesh and a cleavage.

Somewhere, shirt manufacturers were economising on vast rolls of cloth and building houses in Virginia Water. Those discarded shirt tails could have clothed the heathen in mini-skirts – which were also in vogue at the time...a disturbing recollection for those of us who had to climb Blackfriars steps in the wake of the fashionable but overweight office-bound London typist.

Then came the 'pink' shirt for men. Joyce bought me one. Shirts should be white, grey or navy-blue. I wore it with an air of unspoken protest, aware of her watchful eye. She watched me narrowly, alert for insurrection.

Then 'floral shirts' came into vogue. They were a fraction longer in the tail, which was all the excuse she needed. I was dragged into the world of contemporary fashion. She bought me one and offered it up against my chest as if wall-papering a bedroom – which she might well have been. 'Roses. Yellow bloody roses, front, back and all over the meagre tail,' I said.

'You should have bought me a handbag and matching accessories as well!'

'Too much to expect you to say "thank you",' she said, miffed.

I had to go to Glasgow to give a talk at a Yacht Club, which meant that they had to put me up for the night. This usually meant the spare room in somebody's home, a 2 am tiptoe to find the loo, standing on the dog, 'Who's there?' 'Don't move!' I was relieved to find myself delivered to a Temperance Hotel.

A woman insisted on carrying my bag upstairs. She had a bleak and forbidding eye. I babbled something about the weather, which was lousy and she grunted. Or it might have been a growl and I was glad I wasn't wearing the floral shirt, which carried overtones of depravity.

When I got back from my talk and collected my key from the cuddy. She had her lips folded inboard. 'Ye're *alone then*!' she grated, which isn't easy with lips turned in.

When I reached my room I found that my pyjamas were laid out on one side of the bed and that shirt was on the other!

32

The Boggin Line
The rich vocabulary of the sea

Keith and I became sailing-mates because of the hellish racket my engine kicked up. In addition to the usual bangs and splutters of combustion there was the vibration. When in gear, onlookers saw three of everything like out-of-focus 3-D. The galley tinkled and chimed in syncopation from any item in contact with anything else, drawers chattered and the lid of the loo bucket kept up a steady booming like a mating Bittern.

In addition to this cacophony came the gearbox which was 'straight-through' and the work of a madman, like the rest of that sorry conversion. Any change of gear brought a grinding and clashing of tortured metal causing listeners to cry out to their Maker in torment.

To Keith, who was an aircraft engineer, it was like the bellowing of the rutting stag to the ear of the stalker – a challenge. The first time Keith heard my engine, his fine head came up and his nostrils flared. He shuddered perceptibly. He couldn't wait to lay his hands on it.

There had been an earlier contender, a sea-angler named George who heard it and offered to 'look at it', hinting at occult powers of the basilisk sort, in exchange for a day out in Sea Reach where codling were said to be in dizzy abundance.

We anchored, then we rolled and rolled with everything sliding and clattering and me puking. George fished away happily. His bait-box and his lunch-box slid to and fro as if country dancing, with his hand stabbing down on cheese-and-tomato, a whisker away from squirming lugworm and writhing rag. He caught damn-all.

Let's give a cheer for the yard engineer,
A man of gymnastical merit;
As he squirms like an eel, working by feel,
In a space that would cripple a ferret.

Keith and I were fellow club members. He worked at Southend

Airport and had heard that I was due to fly to Paris for the boat show.

'What Company?' he asked.

'So-and-so Airways,' I said.

'Oh,' Keith said. Nothing more, just 'Oh'.

'What do you mean, "Oh"?'

He shook his head. 'Nothing really,' he said in a voice vibrant with falsehood, '*They're probably a good little outfit* – now!' He added, 'Just a tip. Watch out for loose wing rivets and if you see one, tell the stewardess.'

'Oh I will, I will, and thanks for the tip,' I said. Friends like Keith were special. I watched that goddam wing like a cat at a mousehole and I saw a vibrating rivet and told the stewardess. She thanked me and gave me a boiled sweet.

Keith said he'd like to 'look at my engine'. George's inspection and tinkering had proved fair exchange for no codling so I put *Cygnet* alongside. Keith arrived with his tool-box and a glittering eye – a surgeon eyeing the owner of the gall bladder. He checked plugs and magneto and blew through the jets, which was the equivalent of checking blood pressure, heart, lungs and the state of the bowels.

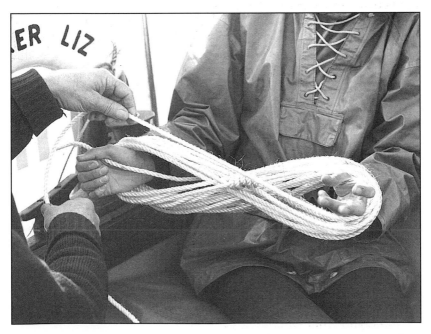

Headless Keith modelling a cat's cradle. This system ensures that the line will run out with two dozen half-hitches in it.

'Let's see what we've got,' he said unwisely. He grasped the starting handle, found compression and swung. He swung about fifty times with endless permutations of choke and throttle setting but the engine remained as dead as a flat hedgehog.

Right on top of the engine block there was a little brass tap called 'a bleeder', which when opened, allowed excess air to escape from the cooling system in case of an air-lock. In keeping with the rest of that sorry conversion, it was the work of a maniac.

'Let's open our bleeder', Keith said.

'Yes, let's open our bleeder,' I concurred. It had absolutely nothing to do with whether or not the engine would start. So we had an open bleeder and a full throttle. The throttle consisted of a screwed rod and a knurled nut which required countless revolutions to move the throttle from closed to open.

Keith swung the handle and the engine exploded into life. It went off like a cracker. One moment cold and inert, next moment flat out;

Cygnet, *our little gaff cutter. Her engine was a conversion from God-knew-what, and my mate Keith regarded it as a challenge. The gear lever went forward for reverse – see what I mean?*

a howling, shrieking, dancing, crazy thing. The boat shook, we shook and our dewlaps rattled.

There was no 'off' switch; there wouldn't be. It would be only a matter of seconds before that nautical scrap-heap disintegrated into a hail of flying components. The bleeder, on top form, shot forth a jet of rust that copped Keith square in the hooter. There he was howling and cursing, trying to snatch off plug leads with electric shocks shooting through him. It was like the birth of Frankenstein. He should have had a ⅝th bolt stuck through his jaw. Professional training won the day. He whacked a screwdriver athwart the HT leads and shorted it out.

The episode forged a link between us; Keith, me and my sodding engine. From that time onwards he never referred to it as anything but 'your sodding engine', as one might refer to a dangerous dog that should by rights be put down, but failing this sensible option, kept at bay and muzzled. It was by way of making amends to him that I suggested he should take out the boat on his own when I couldn't get away.

One of my jobs on *Yachts and Yachting* was to compile a regular feature called 'A to Z', an ongoing lexicon of obscure nautical terms such as Molgogger and Timonoggy, Dandy-wink and Jeer-block. I became almost fanatical about the revival of sea-English, a sort of mouth-to-mouth resuscitation which I practised in my own sailing. Hence the boggin-line.

A boggin-line is a lashing from a rudder blade to a cleat on a side deck; it braces against a tiller lashing to stop a rudder from banging around; wearing pintle and gudgeon. I told Keith clearly and plainly. I said, 'Don't forget your *boggin-line* before you let go the mooring!' You can't be plainer than that.

'Yeah,' he says, 'OK, OK!'

I heard about it from some prod-nose from the club who saw what happened. If anybody is about to make a cock of something, you can guarantee old prod-nose will be watching.

Keith set the mainsail and sheeted the jib aback, looked left and right, cast off the mooring buoy and walked aft with a touch of nonchalance. He would have done better to have run like hell. The boat fell astern to starboard under the combined influence of a backed jib and a rudder hard over to port, held rigidly by the invisible boggin-line.

Prod-nose had never seen nothing like it, never! The boat tacked and gybed in a welter of flogging sails and cracking sheets, sagging to leeward, while Keith hopped and howled, wrenching at the tiller, ducking the flying boom and tearing his hair out. He finally ran forward and heaved the anchor overboard. His eventual discovery of the boggin-line brought a fresh outburst of vituperation in which I figured prominently.

As I say, we had become sailing-mates.

33

An Inventive Streak
My Anker-Yanker folded up like a deckchair

My father had one success, although most of his inventions were fearsome failures. They were fearsome and they usually failed. Not all though; take his specimen-holder mousetrap, a proper little gem, also his cardboard flip-up visor. Oh I could go on and on.

He used to sketch pictures of wild flowers on Sunday evenings after his weekly nature ramble and he'd bring back droopy specimens to draw by the bubbling overhead gas light and hence the visor.

The mousetrap holder was multi-angle and took up half the table, leaving little room for my toy soldiers. He'd clip his specimen at the right angle, put on his Shredded Wheat card visor with the flip-up headband and the visor in the raised position.

'Ha-ha-ha-ha-ha-ha!' I'd cackle, this representing automatic weapon fire, signalling the demise of toy soldiers who fell while still in the standing-aim or kneeling attitude.

'Keep still, don't rock the table Desmond!' he would admonish and his flip-up visor would flip down on the bridge of his nose with a satisfying crack. Which was probably what awakened my interest in inventing things. I got it from him.

Another of his inventions was what mother called the 'tongue-twister'. Father was a Choral Society tenor and he practised 'voice-production' which meant that he sat at the piano holding his guts with one hand, poking the keyboard with a spare finger and singing 'Ahhhhhhh!' on different notes. Alternatively, he had this thing like a little fork which he'd made from plywood, painted an ominous black and with which he held down his tongue while 'Ahhhing'. Once when alone I had a go with it. I made a strangled, choking row because I was strangling and choking.

'My God, my God!' mother cried, rushing in. Then she spotted the tongue-twister and was not well pleased.

He had been an engineer of the belt-driven, overhead shafting genre, Whitworth threaded with a whiff of steam – which was regrettable. For my tenth birthday he bought us a model steam engine, upright like a bottle with a brass boiler and an ominously prominent safety-valve. It had a methylated spirit lamp to boil the water, thus providing fire, boiling water and live steam. Apart from a cut-throat razor, what better gift for a 10-year old lad?

We stood it on an old newspaper to protect the table and father over-filled it with both water and meths. For mother's benefit, having caught the look in her eye, he showed me how to mop up the excess of both. He lit it. We waited. It just sat there and stank. After a long, long while it began to hiss. 'It won't be long now!' father said

Yachting Monthly ran a competition for readers. Invent a thing for recovering halliards which have run aloft. 'Bertie the Biter' was the winner. HRH inspected and approved.

encouragingly and gave the flywheel a poke. The flywheel was a lead casting. It suddenly disappeared in a blur. 'Chchchchchc' it went. We cheered.

'Look, look, look,' I cried needlessly. Oh what a splendid toy! It was rocking and snorting, stink and steam in abundance. The safety-valve started to shriek. Then it happened.

The lamp boiled over and brewed up; the flywheel melted and became elliptical in shape which caused a massive imbalance. Like a miniature steam Darlek, spouting flame and steam, it began strutting around the table as if it owned the joint. The newspaper went up. There was mother howling about 'My table, my table!' father yelling 'Stand back, stand back!' and swiping at it. Then he wrapped the whole goddam thing in a mat and raced out into the garden like an Olympic athlete carrying the torch. 'Great present!' I thought.

After that it was Meccano for me. There was a slogan, 'The Meccano boy of today is the engineer of tomorrow', which implied a world held together with nuts and bolts and riddled with holes like some nightmare gorgonzola. It would be crowded with perforated Forth Bridges and Eiffel Towers. Passengers in jumbo jets would sit with their collars turned up in a howling draught. I learned about sprockets and worm-drives. A worm may turn a pinion but a pinion may not turn a worm. What better training could there be for a lad of limited prospects?

Upon reaching manhood I put aside childish things and invented an object for which there would be little demand and less future, but which might appeal to some no-hoper who couldn't afford a proper anchor winch either. I called it The Anker-Yanker.

It was a break-out lever. When you pull up your anchor, it not infrequently refuses to let go of the seabed. You have a foul anchor. You heave at it from all directions, and if you have a wife, she reminds you that children are listening and that she will not tolerate *that word* and do you hear her?

Quite simply the Yanker was a lever that socketed into the deck, beneath the anchor chain, which it gripped. Each movement of the lever won a few inches of chain. There was a ratchet and a devil's claw, rollers and things. First, I needed a working prototype, so I went and had a yarn with Ollie at the garage.

He had a large belly over which he wore an unbelted brown boiler suit and he looked like a badly stuffed soft toy. He pushed up his welder's mask. It stuck up like the lid of a box containing a particularly disagreeable assortment of features, not least of which was a strawberry nose and a stained moustache like an unwhipped rope's end. I explained what I wanted. He listened attentively.

'What you need, squire, is a li-norler.'

I had never heard of li-norlers and said so.

He clicked tongue-and-teeth with annoyance at such ignorance.

He explained, speaking slowly as one does to half-wits, that it involved a scrap back axle and a take-off from my engine – which being a mechanical blasphemy in its own right gave ominous promise of an engineering nightmare. It would have filled my boat with rattling drive shafts, universal joints, worms and pinions.

My refusal left him a broken man but, rallying, he took a stub of chalk from behind an ear and produced what I wanted. He said I'd have done better with a proper li-norler but there you are. He slammed down his welder's mask and disappeared behind a pyrotechnic display of fizzing sparks which terminated further intercourse.

It worked on my mooring chain a treat! I spent a weekend up and down the creeks Anker-Yanking wherever there were people watching – for advance publicity was essential. My wife Joyce, tight-

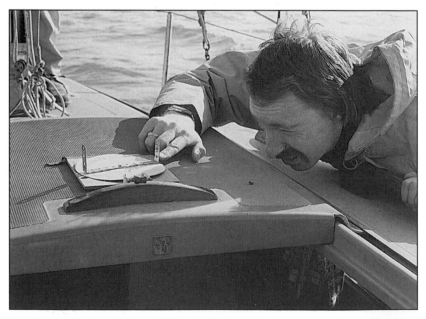

Colin Jarman modelling a bit of bent Meccano with one finger and an eye shut. He responded to treatment, steroids and a low-calorie diet.

lipped, kept below. I invited people to try it and it made a deep impression on them. Mainly on their right-hand thumbs. 'Bloody contraption!' they cried laughingly, holding up blackened thumbnails, hopping around, sucking them. I could see a future for my invention.

I took it to a Patent's Agent who relieved me of fifty quid and awarded me a Provisional Patent which entitled me to put 'Pat applied for' on my literature. A World Patent would come a bit pricey he said, neither would it stop some far eastern pirate from copying and flooding the market with Anker-Yankers! I could imagine it. They'd be packaged with a label showing happy Asiatic faces, laughing dementedly as they hauled up bamboo anchors with instructions in ten languages. Take it from me, Pat would be applied for and no messing.

There was much to be done: a press release, photos, demonstrations, retailers, wholesalers. I must get costings done on a stainless steel version; the mild steel prototype being by that time rusty as a bedstead in a hedge. I never managed any of it and thus avoided the worst financial debacle since investment in brass fly buttons.

I used my Yanker all that season without a failure, and lent it freely to any who wished to test it for themselves, thus ensuring a ready sale in due course. It became a topic for conversation at club bars throughout Essex.

'Seen Sleightholme's new Anker-Yanker?' would come the cry.

'Yes,' would come the laughing rejoiners and blackened thumbs would be up-raised in salute. The end of my dream came abruptly.

There came a day in October when a strong gale was blowing, and *Cygnet* on her mooring was rearing and snatching and rolling her guts out. I thought, 'ideal test' what more could I need? Perhaps a brain scan, the brisk use of a patella hammer and a psychiatrist's couch might have done for starters.

Predictably, getting aboard was hell's own job. Seamanship at its finest. The pram dinghy was tiny. Moses in his basket had twice the leg room. Spray flew as my paddles whipped the waves to a frenzy. I picked my way out through snarling breakers, got alongside, rolled aboard, hitched the painter on aft and went forward on hands and knees. *Cygnet* was chucking it about.

On the tiny foredeck it was like perching on a tea-trolley but without the cress sandwiches and assorted fancies. The bowsprit was smacking down on the seas, and in the bow fairlead the mooring chain graunched and ground. I inserted my Yanker, being careful to keep my thumb erect, tightened my grip and heaved. *Cygnet*, dead on cue rose to a wave then came down like a gardener's boot on a slug. The lever was wrenched out of my hold, a pawl went zinging into space, CRASH went the lever. The Anker-Yanker folded up like a deckchair.

34

Soundings

Twin keels and a teaspoon on a string

The shoal-water yachtsman tends to become wary and suspicious, a consequence of being tricked repeatedly as to the depth of the water, which is coffee-coloured whether it be six feet or six inches in depth. He watches the land, five miles astern, grow misty with distance.

'Farewell dear country,' he sobs brokenly. 'Oh when shall I tread thy blessed acres again?'

In about ten seconds most probably, when his keel drives juddering into Kentish Knock or some other benighted offshore sandbank. Clutching the unshipped tiller, victim of momentum, he gallops forward into thin air and the waiting hatchway.

Years of sailing the clear, deep waters of the south-west, where sea-bed crustacea has no private life whatsoever and a draught of ten feet keeps its head down, had left me unprepared for the Thames Estuary.

Despite now having a draught of only three feet, I continued to sound my way everywhere and still ran aground. Bowing to local custom I even resorted to the sounding pole – a weighted ten-foot bamboo pole marked in feet and stowed in the rigging. Inevitably it fell victim to soft mud and I left it sticking up in my wake, an apparent navigational mark to bewilder the novice. The arrival on the scene of echo sounders merely heightened the problem. Tales of misuse by novices abounded.

'Let me know when it shows two fathoms, Norman.'

There is a lurching crash. 'It's still only one fathom,' says Norman, daft as a rubber nail.

We progressed from one shoal-draught boat to another. Being on a drying mooring meant that the smaller your draught, the longer you were afloat per tide. The boat lay on her ear until the flood tide lifted her, then off you went, sailing frenziedly up, down and around for maybe three hours until the ebb was well away and the rush began to get back on your mooring before you got stranded halfway.

It was like the magic toybox. The clock strikes midnight and the toys, which have been helling it up without restraint, sudddenly hurl themselves back into the box. The lid slams.

The introduction of Napoleon's Revenge, the metric system, merely worsened the sufferings of shoal-draught yachtsmen who now counted on their fingers and *then* ran aground.

We bought a twin-keeler. I got a special discount as an editor. We bought her at the Boat Show which meant that we never got a proper look at her, what with the potted-palms and pebbles. We named her *Miss-Print*, a touch of whimsy, enough to make strong men gag. The first time we were able to stand back and take a good look at her was when we put her on the mooring.

'We should have called her Miss-take!' Joyce said.

Oh we must go down to the sea again,
The key is under the mat;
We'd prefer a square-rigger,
Being safer and bigger,
But we'll just have to put up with THAT!

At twenty-four feet in length, perched up on her keels, plump and a bit squat she looked like some old woman in a bus queue – plastic mac and sensible shoes, with two bags of shopping and varicose veins, longing to sit down. The deed was done.

All of which is unjustified and a wicked calumny: she turned out to be a bouncy, jolly little boat that carried us safely to and fro across the North Sea, with a dry deck and a forecabin in which our by then teenage daughter and her mates could rant and rail in private about grown-up domination and It's Not Fair.

Twin keels though are something else. Twin keels are supposed to make drying out a pleasure and a convenience combined with the advantages of shoal draught, a go-anywhere concept and no worries on arrival about finding space to anchor. You just find a bit of clear mud *and stop*.

Drying out upright was a luxury. Trying to brew a pot of tea in a boat which is lying at an angle of around forty degrees has all the charm of pup-tent camping, of spinal agony and cowpats – crawling around like a beetle and trying to pour a jet of tea at seemingly right angles to the mug. Twin keels remedies all that. What it doesn't remedy is the problem of running aground.

Me modelling a biker's helmet. With earflaps down it made me look like a St Bernard. I bought it at Millets who also sold war surplus gas trousers and Greek railway fog-horns.

In a boat with a conventional keel, running aground is usually dealt with by heeling the boat to reduce her draught. With twin keels, heeling her merely digs one keel in deeper; you have to try to keep her bolt upright. Reducing weight is your only last hope. You pile all unwanted souls into the dinghy alongside and forget to make fast the painter. Or father gets overboard and shoves – and gets left behind.

Lulled into a state of upright euphoria, these finer points escaped my attention. We went weekend cruising up the Essex creeks; me, Joyce and our small daughter, a happy family party, give-or-take a bit of belly-aching about it being *boring* and will there be shops?

The weather deteriorated, became first hazy, then drizzly and then began to squall. We were in for a windy night, where should we go? Anchorages were crowded with moorings. We must dry out I proclaimed, we will find a clear patch of mud and sit on our keels like it says in the brochure.

I found the ideal spot in the mouth of this creek; shallow, uncluttered and free from humps and gullies, perfect drying-out conditions. The wind was gusting hard down the creek, but once we were dried out who cared? A rhetorical question.

I had missed one important factor. Twin keels may either be splayed out like a goalkeeper about to let one through or they may be vertical, a device which means that during building, the glassfibre hull, like a jelly, comes out of its mould more easily. Ours were vertical. And therefore less stable when perched upon, as any bar-stool habitué will testify.

I anchored in nought feet of water and minutes later we were on. Joyce hauled up a bucket of water to use for flushing the loo when the water had left us. I poked around with the boathook and found no humps or gullies, although the mud sloped fairly steeply – a fact which only became apparent when it was much too late for anything to be done about it.

'We're all sideways!' Joyce said.

'Ugh we're all tipped over!' said daughter.

Down below, a man of science, I suspended a teaspoon from the deckhead and down a door post to serve as a simple plumb-bob, thus indicating our angle of heel. It was damn nearly twenty degrees from vertical. A squall howled through our rigging and shook us like a terrier with a rat.

The wind shift came at about 2am, predictably veering west nor'west, and blowing a howling hoolie full on our beam. The boat shuddered. I was out of my bunk, torch in hand, shining it on my plumb-bob. 'I need the loo!' my daughter wailed from up forward. The loo was on the downhill side.

'No, no!' I cried. 'Nobody is to use the loo or we'll be over!'

Twenty-two degrees my plumb-bob read.

So it was all my fault. I was to blame, I was the culprit.

'Oh for heaven's sake!' Joyce said.

The bucket was full of water and could not be used. It was alright for men.

'You'll have to keep your weight on the *up* side while she *goes*!' I pontificated.

And so that awful night passed, me on the plumb-bob, boat shuddering and rocking, girls taking it in turn to act as counter-weights.

The sound of the returning tide, lapping and smacking between those twin keels, was like a symphony concert.

35

Salvage
It seemed a good idea at the time

In the days of sail, the East Coast fishermen combined compassion with the lucrative trade of rescue, which gave birth to the entirely worthy Royal National Lifeboat Service, manned by volunteers which puts the saving of 'souls' above all else.

The nuns at school had taught me about souls. Nuns wear this big white dicky, right? Sister Agnes would put an ink-dot on her dicky. 'That,' she would say, 'is what a *venial sin* on a *soul* looks like.' We would gaze at it with pleasure.

'But if I were to black it *all over*!' she would roar suddenly, rising to her feet with a terrible frown. 'What would it be like?'

'A mortal sin, sister!' we would chant, having known in advance that sinful souls look like inky dickies. None of which has the slightest relevance to salvage but needs to be mentioned in order to put matters straight.

The beach 'yoll' (yawl) crews of the Norfolk coast were masters at the art of lucrative soul-saving and they worked as 'Companies', each with its driftwood hut of which many old photos survive, showing the Yoll crews as booted, with beards like doormats and arms folded, scowling at the cameraman. Keith and I had no ambitions to emulate these fine, albeit hairy men, but sailing on the East Coast involves you in its past.

Take old man Turnidge in Leigh, one of the *old*, old boys who remembered things. I once asked him about the scandalous case of the schooner wrecked on a sandbank, how the fishermen of Southend had taken off her crew, then gone back and nicked every last inch of her running rigging. He drew himself up to his full height, trembling with fury, flinty of eye.

'A wicked lie!' he cried in his old man's treble, chin wobbling.

I said that I'd read it in a book.

'Tis lies, lies! She weren't no schooner, she wuz a ketch!'

My mate Keith and I had occasional muddy weekend cruises,

dedicated to hunting out the muddy history of the Thames Estuary and its bawlie-men and barging sailormen. One of our favourite jaunts being the circumnavigation of the Isle of Sheppey, which involves you in a spot of coastal pilotage plus a very great deal of mud.

Sheppey is an island by virtue of the river Swale, which is not a river at all but a tidal moat that lops off a bit of Kent east of the Medway, which *is* a river. Midway there is a tidal node where two streams meet head-on and a fair becomes a foul tide.

There is also Kingsferry lifting rail/road bridge which involves a variety of flashing lights and family tension over the starting or the refusal to start of engines. Cursing, impatient motorists rap steering wheels and yachts manoeuvre in tight circles awaiting a train or, upon rounding a bend and seeing that the bridge is open, motor flat out in the vain hope of it remaining that way. Red lights flash. 'Typical!' sob skippers, 'Bloody typical!' The Kingsferry bridge is always good value.

Kingsferry lifting bridge on the Swale in Kent, scene of some of the ripest language known to man. Motorists cursed yachtsmen who cursed the bridge-man who cursed the lot of them.

There is also Queenborough, once a royal route to the Continent but when I knew it, it was lying under a constant cloud of stink and fat, happy flies from a glue factory; the flies fortunately now emancipated and the factory restored to its ancient charm. When circumnavigating Sheppey, either east-about or west-about we usually stopped at 'Pongborough' as it was then known to many, to 'take aboard stores and provisions', which being liquid went aboard but briefly.

On the occasion of our merciful salvage attempt we were going east-about in *Cygnet* and having crossed the Thames, we were heading for Four Fathom Channel. There was this little boat ahead, rolling her guts out, beam-on, almost rolling her gun'les under. There was nobody aboard her.

'Bloody angler's boat!' Keith identified with difficulty, since he was using my binoculars which appeared to have a nest of tarantulas in them.

Anglers' boats of the pre-plastics age were like no other. They were the *least* boat you could get away with. They were the boats that everybody else had written off as unrepairable. Boats to an angler were merely fishing platforms, to be kept afloat by any means. They also had a windbreak stuck up like the hood of a pram only in plywood, the sort of cuddy erected by workmen at a hole in the road. I had seen one such lamentable craft with navigation lights made from fish-paste jars painted all-round red and green, and which must have been the occasion for many a gear lever hauled from forward to aft in one cursing sweep and many a helm banged hard upon the stops, accompanied by howls for justice.

This boat had no such refinements. The water in her sloshed; floorboards floated. Her inventory appeared to be basic, consisting of two empty bottles of India Pale Ale, export strength.

'She's a write off.' Keith summed up, a bit brutally, whereupon I took umbrage and in so-doing gave us both a lot of grief.

'She's probably some poor man's pride-and-joy,' I said prissily. 'All some poor chap can afford, which is why we're going to salvage her!'

Keith put on his disagreeable face.

'I'll lay alongside her but you'll need to be quick!' I told him.

'Now hang on,' he said.

There was no time for debate, I thrust a bucket into his hands and yelled 'Now!' He landed kneeling and filled both his boots. I circled for ten minutes while he baled, then I chucked him the towrope which he secured with difficulty by reason of having to crawl through the cuddy. He came aboard squelching and in a thunderous mood.

'This boat is probably some poor chap's prize possession,' I said reprovingly. 'Apart from dry bloody boots!' Keith griped.

It was like towing a brick wall. We were heading back for the mouth of the Medway and each jerk brought us up solid, so I put the engine on, which makes it sound like some sort of Freemason's apron, but which made steering possible. The tow was sheering from side to side like a supermarket trolley, so I put Keith back aboard her with an oar to steer her. His eye-rolling should have broken my heart.

We had reached the dredged channel, shaping up for Garrison Point, when I became aware that he was yelling and waving. Thinking that he must be applauding my consummate boat-handling skill, I bowed and made a think-nothing-of-it gesture, but his agitation increased and he was pointing at my stern.

I looked over. The exhaust exit which also carried the cooling

water was jetting steam, no water. I cut the engine dead. I hauled Keith alongside. He lifted the lid of the engine box and there was a heavy waft of oil and heat. I was fortunate in having him, a trained engineer aboard. He summoned up a mouthful of saliva and gobbed expertly at the engine block which sizzled and spat.

'It'll be *hours* before we dare start that again!' he said with relish. The ebb was beginning to run out of the Medway. We managed to get in one tack across to Grain Island and then crabbed back to the lee of Garrison Point where I dumped anchor and brought up on the very edge of the shallows. An early dusk was setting in. We should have been in the pub at Harty Ferry by now. We cooked supper, gobbed at the engine, brewed tea and gobbed and kept gobbing. I suspected that Keith was setting me up. It was pitch black and very cold. Once a searchlight reached out from the Garrison and picked us over as a fussy diner might poke around with his fork.

At last the ebb began to slacken and the engine was stone cold albeit messy on top. Keith cranked her up and we began to head into the river for Sheerness. There was a commercial dock in which pleasure craft were not welcomed but since nobody in his wildest, most fevered dreams would ever have associated 'pleasure' with the sorry heap we were towing, I headed for the entrance.

There was nobody about to thank us for our merciful work. We left her moored by some steps and I pinned a note to the cuddy. It read, 'With compliments from well-wishers. No salvage will be claimed.' I signed it and added my address, for plainly some poor fellow would want to write and thank me. Glowing with good works – even Keith showed signs of pride in our feat of seamanship – we motored the short distance to Queenborough and anchored for the rest of the night.

A reply to my note arrived within days. It read as follows.

'This boat must be removed within seven days pending a penalty of £50 (fifty pounds).'

It was signed The Harbourmaster.

36

(Right) Up the Creek
A muddy playground for all ages

Other people were girdling the world, watching the dawn come up like thunder in Mandalay and the sun go down off Viti Levu while I was stuck on the mud up Paglesham Creek.

I could never count on longer than two consecutive weeks holiday per annum, and at three and a half knots flat out it limits your range a bit. I don't knock the old Maurice Griffiths concept though, the creek-to-creek adventures that all end up snug at anchor with a spatter of rain on deck, the cabin lamp burning bright and bangers sizzling in the pan.

So we bumped our weekend way up and down that shoal-water coast and the curlews and red-shanks muttered and piped as the tide flooded the saltings. You don't *have* to have a boat filled with electronics and sail marina-to-marina, credit card in hand, to enjoy cruising and it isn't how far you go, it is how much you put into it that makes it fun.

I met a family cruiser coming out of the Walton Backwaters; the owner leaned on his tiller contentedly sucking his pipe while an uncountable number of muddy kids towed astern in two muddy dinghies. He gave me a wry grin.

'Arthur-bloody-Ransome weekend!' he said.

We all had dry moorings, boats laid on their ears between tides, unusable or at such an angle that being down below was like one of those amusement arcade 'Krazy Kottages' where everything is crooked and a mechanical voice goes, 'Ho, ho, ho!' You can't even use the loo without defying gravity – which did Newton no good either. It was hardly surprising then that when weekend cruising, our objective was to anchor and remain gloriously upright. Since all the old, traditional anchorages were becoming choked with rows of moorings, this meant finding new ones.

Three feet of draught was about the maximum. There are holes left behind at low tide in which a boat of modest draught can just manage to lie afloat trussed fore-and-aft between anchors but afloat and cut off from all contact with the world of men.

There the mud connoisseur can watch as others, seeing him at anchor, attempt to follow. Any moment now, he muses, watching the approaching mast with relish. It stops abruptly and then genuflects. Distantly comes the howl of an engine full astern.

There was one particular hole that I came upon at the mouth of a gully that went nowhere. At even the lowest of low waters there remained just enough water to accommodate our three feet of draught and I had an idea. Why not spend a whole season moored there, upright?

When we bought *Cygnet* she came complete with anchor and chain as was to be expected. This anchor however was a forty pound Danforth, which for a boat of only twenty-two feet in length was equivalent, in terms of security, to wearing brick trousers. We *never* dragged. We lay up-and-down in the smallest of areas and snubbed wickedly when anything went by, but not an inch did she drag.

I placed this splendid anchor exactly in the middle of the hole and the boat lay to it all that season. When we went sailing I buoyed and left it behind and used our kedge as a bower. It was legal. You're

allowed to leave your anchor. Had I been less trusting, I might have wondered why nobody nicked it.

When I tried to raise it at laying-up time I found out. I couldn't *move it*! So I waited until low tide, hauled it up taut and 'hung' it off with a rope lashing, which was very fortunate and to my credit if nothing else was.

The flood tide came stealing in, trickling and gurgling, fat chocolate bubbles – on the East Coast the water is the colour of drinking chocolate. The anchor chain became bar-rigid, it graunched in the fairlead. The bows remained down and our stern rose. So did the tide.

I chickened out when the foredeck had six inches of freeboard left and the rudder was out of the water. My knife seemed only to brush the lashing and it went off like a cracker. I went base-over-apex. I got a fishing boat to lift my anchor and it had a bend in the shank that I never managed to straighten.

Next season some other son-of-a-bitch got there first. Come the autumn when he tried to lift his hook I missed what happened, but others didn't and it became folklore. He waited until his bow was well down and then ran aft. This transference of weight proved effective. Up came the anchor, down went the stern and he just went on running.

On the southeast coast you occasionally get 'storm surge'. When a series of heavy gales from the nor-west occur in the northern North Sea, the funnel-effect as the waters narrow, drives up the height of tide in the southern North Sea. Houseboats far inland with roses round the gangplank get a letterbox full of mud and crab's legs. Storm surge gave rise to another bit of folklore.

There was this yachtsman who went off on a single-handed weekend cruise around the creeks. His wife said it would do him a world of good to unwind, commune with nature and recharge his batteries, in a manner of speaking. Which is a fair description of the benefits he was to enjoy, aided by his secretary whom he picked up clandestinely from a secluded landing somewhere up the Medway, heading thereafter to a mud hole and guaranteed solitude.

On the very top of the tide he floated in, moored immovably, then unwound, recharged his batteries and certainly communed with nature. Then at high water next day he tried to motor out of his love-nest.

He was stuck hard-on. The tide had 'cut'.

There were no mobile phones then. There was no way of getting out on foot. There was no way of getting out at all! A six-foot pram dinghy is not the best of vehicles for undertaking a row of interminable length through a maze of muddy gullies, besides which it started raining and she was adamant.

He tried again without success on the night high water, and again on Monday, but the water failed to reach the height it had reached on the storm surge.

His wife, worried by his non-appearance, phoned the police and then the Coastguard, who notified the search-and-rescue helicopter which over-flew the area and, armed with a description of the yacht, came up with the best possible news.

'Your husband *and the young lady* appear to be quite safe and well, madam,' said the Coastguard, harbinger of glad tidings, setting her mind at rest.

'Safe and well is he!' she grated. 'He'll be neither once I get my hands on him!'

On the Medway marshes. It was said to be a winding-engine for hauling taut a cable boom across the river to thwart Dutch invaders, which is a lousy trick. 'Bum? What bum? I see no bum. Carry on bosun!'

37

The Beam Reach
A night to remember

I know what heaven is like, I've been there.

We locked out of Flushing, which is aptly named seeing that we were flushed out with a bundle of barges and a score of yachts, straight into the Westerschelde, wind-over-tide and a sea like a field of bricks. We motor-sailed bang, bang, bang for hours, spray and breakfasts flying and a North Sea crossing to come. That bit was hell rather than heaven or a pretty vile spell of purgatory. A 'purging' it surely was.

The day ground on. We dropped the land astern, which is to say that the murk diluted into uniform grot but at least the sea eased and *Tinker Liz* picked up the tune and fell into step; I put her on the steering vane. By dusk, we were over the humps and bumps and I could see Noord Hinder giving me the eye, two every ten seconds under the foot of the jib. Joyce didn't want any supper so I let her sleep, she'd had a rough day. I had a dose of Scotch then some soup and wuffed some bread, then I sailed into heaven.

There was a full moon, the breeze came aft force four on the beam and the little yacht stretched, reached forward and started to go. It wasn't *that* fast, five touching an occasional six knots maybe, but she *purred*, no thump, no splash, she just lay curve-to-curve and wash-to-wake, one with the other like young lovers lying together under the moon.

The sea softened into silk sheets. Hour after hour she slipped along with the vane nudging her and the phosphorescence bursting in fireworks from rudder and keel. Should I wake Joyce so that she could know the marvel of it? She snored very softly and swayed to the gentle roll. No, best not.

The moon rose to her apogee, and began her long descent down the starry staircase. A few ships lumbered by. I felt no weariness, my pipe smoked sweetly and the bow and stern waves whispered and tinkled. Now and again the prop began turning thud, thud, thud, then, abashed by its mechanical temerity, it would fall silent again. The myriad buoy lights of the southern North Sea were like fireflies on a summer's night.

How often did I brew a mug of tea that long night? Each tasted sweeter than the last – feet up, pipe going, swing and sway with that old moon trailing a silver serpent athwart our way.

The night melted and astern the sky split in a golden rend, then orange and mary-blue and the dawn came up. I had expected to see a lightship ahead, I *needed* to see it. We had crossed the tail of the Galloper, seen Outer Gabbard but where was the Sunk?

A sour note after such a sail, a small worry but I need not have worried for this was a magic night. The Sunk Lightship was hidden from my view by the service vessel that lay alongside her. Joyce stuck a mug of tea into my fist.

'You should have called me!' she said.

Glossary

Abaft: Behind, eg abaft the mast.

All fours: Tied up, moored with four ropes.

All standing: An abrupt stop.

At the run: Without a stop.

Athwart: Across, eg athwart the deck.

Backs: The wind shifts anticlockwise.

Beam: Breadth of a boat.

Bow: The front of the boat.

Brails: Lines that gather a sail like a curtain.

Bring up: To stop, usually at anchor.

Broach: Driven sideways.

Bulls eyes: Spherical blocks; rope guides.

Careening: Heeling a moored boat to expose the bottom.

Clinker: A construction method in which planks overlap (usually the hull of a boat).

Close hauled: Heading into the wind with all sail in tight.

Crabbed: Crabbing, a sideways drift.

Crosstree(s): Lateral mast bracing struts.

Dagger board: A lifting keel.

Dipping lug: An almost square sail. The front top edge is passed round the mast when tacking.

Echo sounder: Electronic instrument recording depth of water.

Fantail: Sloping end of the stern.

Fended off: Pushed away from, eg a fender (which protects the sides of the boat from hard objects).

Fo'c's'le: Fore-castle (historic). The fore part of the ship below deck.

Force ten: Wind of storm force ie around 50 knots.

Freeboard: Height of hull above the water.

Fore reach: Forward and sideways drift.

Gaff mainsail: Four-sided as opposed to triangular shaped mainsail.

Gribble: A wood-boring insect harmful to ship's hull.

Grid compass: Course steered is kept between parallel lines.

Gybe: Changing the boat's direction while heading downwind (ie with the wind coming from behind the boat).

Guardrails: A wire rope, safety 'fence' around the deck edge.

Gudgeon: Rudder hinge, eg an eye fitting over a 'pintle' or spike.

Gunn'les: Gun-wales. Upper edge of a boat's sides.

Hard on the wind/ closehauled: Heading into the wind (ie when the wind is coming from the front of the boat).

Heading: Direction the boat is sailing in.

Holding ground: Seabed as a

hold for an anchor, good, poor etc.

Hove-to: Forward progress arrested by adjusting the angle of the sails.

Hull: The actual body of the boat excluding mast, superstructure, rig rudder.

Kedge: A light anchor.

Ketch rig: Two-masted. The smaller 'rear' mast is forward of the rudder.

Knot: Measurement of boat/ windspeed.

Lanyard: A short rope/line for a bucket, etc.

Leading marks: Shore features/ marks kept in a line to guide the boat into a channel.

Leadline: A marked plumb-line (rope) used to measure the depth of water.

Lee: Downwind side eg lee sheet, lee rail, lee side.

Log: An instrument, electronic or mechanical, recording distance sailed through the water. Ship's record book.

Luff: Forward edge of a sail. To luff: to head a boat directly into the wind so the boat will slow down.

Miss stays: An intended tack (turn) through the wind that only gets half-way.

Mizzen: The aftermost mast and sail.

Moor: To secure a boat to the shore/mooring buoy etc, using lines/ropes.

Mud berth: A gully on marshland where a boat can be moored.

Neaped: Stranded between a high 'spring' and lesser 'neap' tide.

Nock: The front upper corner of a gaff sail.

Opening up: Holes in a wooden hull caused by drying and shrinkage.

Overfall: Rough water due to fast tidal current usually over rocks.

Parbuckle: One end of a rope is made fast; the other is taken down beneath an object that is cylindrical eg a spar, and up to the crew who raises the object by hauling the line.

Paying off: When a sailing vessel heads off away from where the wind is coming from.

Peak up: Raise the gaff end (upper outer corner) of a gaff sail.

Pinching: Heading a sailing boat too close to the wind thus losing power.

Pluck: A tow.

Port tack boat: the give-way boat when two boats converge to windward.

Pulpit: Bow and stern safety rails.

Raft: Boats moored side-by-side.

Reach: A stretch of sheltered water.

Reaching: Sailing beam to wind ie the wind blowing on the side of the boat.

Rig: The part of the boat that supports and includes the sail. A sailing boat is described by her rig eg bermudan-rigged.

Rooster-tail: Plume of water thrown up by a propeller.

Rucking: Rumpling, creasing eg 'the nock' or mast/gaff corner of the sail.

Scandalise: Reduce the drive of a gaff sail by raising /dropping corners.

Sea anchor: A canvas 'drag' to hold a ship facing the seas

Sheered off: Moved away in a lateral direction.

Sheerline: The upward curve of a ship's deck and rail.

Shoaling water: Shallowing water.

Shroud: One of a set of mast-supporting stays.

Solent tides: a second (slightly lower) high tide an hour later.

Soundings: Reference to charted depths of water.

Spring: A mooring rope spanning the whole length of the vessel.

Spring tides/springs: Tides that occur at or near the time when the moon is full and new. High tides are higher than at other times ie neaps and low tides are lower. Currents are stronger.

Stays: Supports for the mast. In stays: Head-to-wind (so not moving) and without steerage way.

Stern: The back of the boat.

Stopped up: Breaking-stops. Sail stowed thus for quick/easy setting.

Stud-link: Anchor chain link with cross-bar to give strength.

Swim-headed: A barge lighter with blunt, overhanging ends.

Swatchways: East Anglian term. A narrow channel between sandbanks.

Sway aboard: To haul something up and swing it on board.

Tacking: Sailing to windward (ie towards the wind) in a series of zig-zag headings because it is impossible to sail directly into the wind.

Thwarts: Boat seats.

Tide-wind: Becalmed boat. Breeze caused as moved by tidal current.

Tingles: Exterior/interior patches applied to hull planking.

Topping lift: Rope for lifting the end of the boom.

Tow-blocks: Said when a tackle is fully tightened, blocks together.

Under-foot: Anchor dropped straight down to act as a drag.

Veer: Clockwise wind-shift. Let out more anchor cable.

Watch-and-watch: Two crew taking equal and ongoing shifts while the other one sleeps.

Weather window: Brief fine spell in continuous bad weather.

Windward (go to): Driving a boat upwind ie towards where the wind is coming from, beating, tacking.

Wrinkle the nock: hoist the gaff until creases appear in the sail.